Supporting mathematical development in the early years

Supporting early learning

Series Editors: Vicky Hurst and Jenefer Joseph

The focus of this series is on improving the effectiveness of early education. Policy developments come and go, and difficult decisions are often forced on those with responsibility for young children's well-being. This series aims to help with these decisions by showing how developmental approaches to early education provide a sound and positive basis for learning.

Each book recognizes that children from birth to six have particular developmental needs. This applies just as much to the acquisition of subject knowledge, skills and understanding as to other educational goals such as social skills, attitudes and dispositions. The importance of providing a learning environment which is carefully planned to stimulate children's own active learning is also stressed.

Throughout the series, readers are encouraged to reflect on the education being offered to young children, through revisiting developmental principles and using them to analyse their observations of children. In this way, readers can evaluate ideas about the most effective ways of educating young children and develop strategies for approaching their practice in ways which offer every child a more appropriate education.

Published titles:

Vicky Hurst and Jenefer Joseph: *Supporting Early Learning: The Way Forward*
Bernadette Duffy: *Supporting Creativity and Imagination in the Early Years*
Linda Pound: *Supporting Mathematical Development in the Early Years*
Marian Whitehead: *Supporting Language and Literacy Development in the Early Years*

Supporting mathematical development in the early years

Linda Pound

Open University Press
Buckingham • Philadelphia

Open University Press
Celtic Court
22 Ballmoor
Buckingham
MK18 1XW

email: enquiries@openup.co.uk
world wide web:http://www.openup.co.uk
and
325 Chestnut Street
Philadelphia, PA19106, USA

First Published 1999

A catalogue record of this book is available from the British Library

ISBN   0 335 19887 2 (pb)   0 335 19888 0 (hb)

Library of Congress Cataloging-in-Publication Data
Pound, Linda.
   Supporting mathematical development in the early years/Linda Pound.
   p. cm. – (Supporting early learning)
   Includes bibliographical references and index.
   ISBN 0-335-19888-0 (hbk.). – ISBN 0-335-19887-2 (pbk.)
   1. Mathematics–Study and teaching (Early childhood)   I. Title.   II. Series.
QA135.5.P68   1999
372.7'044–dc21
98-49817
CIP

Typeset by Type Study, Scarborough
Printed in Great Britain by Biddles Ltd, Guildford and King's Lynn

Contents

Series editors' preface

This book is one of a series which will be of interest to all those who are concerned with the care and education of children from birth to 6 years old – childminders, teachers and other professionals in schools, those who work in playgroups, private and community nurseries and similar institutions; governors, providers and managers. We also speak to parents and carers, whose involvement is probably the most influential of all for children's learning and development.

Our focus is on improving the effectiveness of early education. Policy developments come and go, and difficult decisions are often forced on all those with responsibility for young children's well-being. We aim to help with these decisions by showing how developmental approaches to young children's education not only accord with our fundamental educational principles, but provide a positive and sound basis for learning.

Each book recognizes and demonstrates that children from birth to 6 years old have particular developmental learning needs, and that all those providing care and education for them would be wise to approach their work developmentally. This applies just as much to the acquisition of subject knowledge, skills and understanding, as to other educational goals such as social skills, attitudes and dispositions. In this series there are several volumes with a subject-based focus, and the main aim is to show how that can be introduced to young children within the framework of an integrated and developmentally appropriate curriculum, without losing its integrity as an area of knowledge in its own right. We also stress the importance of providing a learning environment which is carefully planned for children's own active learning. The present volume addresses the anxieties about mathematics, which still abound, in both adults and children, and offers us a variety of ways in which we can dispel them. The author shows us how quickly and how early on very young children start 'coming to terms' with mathematics, and how adults, both at home and elsewhere, can and should support and extend this early competence.

Access for all children is fundamental to the provision of educational opportunity. We are concerned to emphasize anti-discriminatory approaches throughout, as well as the importance of recognizing that meeting special educational needs must be an integral purpose of curriculum development and planning. We see the role of play in learning as a central one, and one which also relates to all-round emotional, social and physical development. Play, along with other forms of active learning, is normally a natural point of access to the curriculum for each child at his or her particular stage and level of understanding. It is therefore an essential force in making for equal opportunities in learning, intrinsic as it is to all areas of development. We believe that these two aspects, play and equal opportunities, are so important that we not only highlight them in each volume in this series, but also include separate volumes on them as well.

Throughout this series, we encourage readers to reflect on the education being offered to young children, through revisiting the developmental principles which most practitioners hold, and using them to analyse their observations of the children. In this way, readers can evaluate ideas about the most effective ways of educating young children, and develop strategies for approaching their practice in ways which exemplify their fundamental educational beliefs, and offer every child a more appropriate education.

The authors of each book in the series subscribe to the following set of principles for a developmental curriculum:

Principles for a developmental curriculum

- Each child is an individual and should be respected and treated as such.
- The early years are a period of development in their own right, and education of young children should be seen as a specialism with its own valid criteria of appropriate practice.
- The role of the educator of young children is to engage actively with what most concerns the child, and to support learning through these preoccupations.
- The educator has a responsibility to foster positive attitudes in children

to both self and others, and to counter negative messages which children may have received.

- Each child's cultural and linguistic endowment is seen as the fundamental medium of learning.
- An anti-discriminatory approach is the basis of all respect-worthy education, and is essential as a criterion for a developmentally appropriate curriculum (DAC).
- All children should be offered equal opportunities to progress and develop, and should have equal access to good quality provision. The concepts of multiculturalism and anti-racism are intrinsic to this whole educational approach.
- Partnership with parents should be given priority as the most effective means of ensuring coherence and continuity in children's experiences, and in the curriculum offered to them.
- A democratic perspective permeates education of good quality and is the basis of transactions between people.

Vicky Hurst and Jenefer Joseph

Introduction

> We are, all of us, at all ages, already highly skilled mathema-
> ticians. We just haven't often learned it in our mathematics
> lessons.
>
> (Lewis 1996: 17)

Mathematics education is the topic of much heated debate in Britain. Politicians and employers express alarm that our children seem to be doing so
much worse than children in other countries. They clutch at straws, often
suggesting that a return to the methods which failed so large a proportion
of the adult population will somehow be more successful in the future.
Since, the argument goes, Pacific Rim countries and successful European
countries such as Hungary use whole-class teaching for mathematics, that
must be what makes the difference – ignoring the peer tutoring, the later
start to formal schooling and elements of other systems which might be
key contributory factors. The assertion that children's work in Japan may
be more accurate and complex than that of children of a similar age in
Britain is, for example, frequently made. However, the suggestion that it
may lack the investigative and creative flair that the mathematics of many
British children shows is less often made. Parents want their children to
succeed but often have a relatively narrow view of what counts as mathematics. Some of the competence which is essential in a technological age
requires far more than simply an ability to follow instructions for long
division or to learn tables by heart.

Educationalists blame the impact of Piaget's work, which they claim has
been interpreted in such a way as to favour individualized approaches to
learning. They claim, too, that teachers overlook the push to understanding that comes from peer-group discussion and from teacher intervention
which challenges children's thinking. Some blame lack of teacher knowledge, while others suggest that the underlying problem is that as a society

the British do not place a high value on facility with number (Ofsted 1997). Low achievement is a problem which must be tackled. Early childhood specialists share the British concern with low standards but seek also to protect children from the backlash which suggests that the solution is an earlier and more formal start to education.

This book sets out to show how competent young children are and how, if we wish to address low achievement, we should be building on all that children know and achieve in the early years. In this way we can support the achievement of individual children and, in time, of the British nation as a whole.

Chapter 1 gives an overview of young children's mathematical behaviour at home and in early years settings, contrasting that with the sometimes abrupt change that occurs on entry to statutory schooling. In Chapter 2 the characteristics of learning in the early years which have a positive impact on all future learning are examined. In particular, the relationship between mathematics and language learning is considered. The way in which learning is most effective when based on children's 'persistent concerns' (Athey 1990), the role of representation in mathematical learning, mathematical connections (both neurological and in thought itself) and the need for children to develop a positive attitude towards mathematics are all examined. Chapter 3 defines both the content and the learning curriculum (Claxton 1997) required to promote mathematical thinking, and in Chapter 4 issues concerning the implementation of such a curriculum are considered. The role of staff in observing, planning for and supporting children's learning by a variety of strategies is examined in Chapter 5. The importance of a close partnership between the child's parents or principal carer and staff working in early years settings is explored in Chapter 6. Suggestions are made for promoting partnership.

1

Mathematics at home and at school

Mathematics is an important part of our everyday lives. The use of numbers for counting, ordering and quantifying measurements is recognized by all; asking for a specific number of items, turning left at the third set of traffic lights, buying 2 pounds of apples or half a litre of milk, deciding that even though the label says that a jacket is designed for a 6-month-old baby it will be too small for the baby we have in mind, estimating when to cook different dishes so that the whole meal is ready at the same time, and working out whether the cashier has given us the right change when we go shopping are all situations where we use mathematics with varying degrees of confidence. Confusingly for children, we also use numbers as identifying labels – for example telephone, PIN and social security numbers. Notions of shape and space are part of our everyday mathematical understanding, too – working out how much carpet we need in square yards and square metres is one thing, but realizing that a long thin off-cut of carpet will be of less value to us than one which is closer to the squarish shape of the room, even though they are of a similar area, requires a different understanding.

But mathematics is much more than this – if our young children are to become confident and competent users of mathematics for the twenty-first century they will need to learn to recognize mathematics as a powerful tool for communication. Mathematics can help us to solve problems and to identify recurring patterns and themes. Most surprising of all, to some adults and children, is that it can be exciting, creative and enjoyable. Indeed, if it is to be of genuine use to young children growing up today, we must help them to revel in their mathematical thinking, to have confidence in their calculations and estimations and to develop a keen sense of curiosity about the ways in which mathematics touches and enhances our lives. They must develop not only mathematical knowledge, understanding and skills but also a disposition to enjoy learning mathematics. Above all adults must cherish and enhance the intensity, the ecstatic responses, the exuberance and joy which young children bring to their daily life, channelling it to support learning throughout their lives.

It is all too apparent that this is not the reality for most adults. The Cockcroft Report (Department of Education and Science 1982) demonstrated that for many adults, mathematics is a subject to be feared. Many people acknowledged to the investigating team that they could not work out how much the petrol they needed would cost, could not add small sums of money and were often afraid of numbers. Stein (1989: 64, 65), in her study of parents' attitudes to mathematics, quotes parents describing their experiences at school:

I remember having to recite tables at the front of the class and hating it!

I am fairly competent but I can still get frozen by attempting to work out arithmetic in my head.

I never enjoyed maths and could never remember my times tables. I am very bad at maths now – not very competent at all.

Maths was my worst subject! . . . I had a block on maths. I couldn't hold things in my mind and I never understood why. The primary teaching was parrot fashion for tables. Sums were a quick explanation by an authoritarian teacher who was exasperated when I did not get it. I have no confidence in maths. [My maths teacher said] 'You've been a right failure this year . . .! What are you – a right failure!'

In the following sections, the characteristics of children's mathematical development have been outlined. The stated ages are offered only as guidance – children's mathematical development, like so many other aspects of their learning, strongly reflects the culture within which they grow up. Children generally pay most attention to those aspects of a culture which they recognize as having particular significance for the people that are important to them in their day-to-day lives (Rogoff 1990). Moreover, as Clarke and Atkinson (1996: 25) remind us:

Children do not seem to learn maths in a linear way, learning one thing after another. It is a complex process. They often learn things that we don't think we have taught them, and fail to learn things that we think we have taught them. Learning seems to resemble a jigsaw, with concepts clicking into place as new experiences inform previous experiences.

Mathematical thinking from 0 to 3 years of age

From birth, babies show remarkable abilities. Their inclination to work hard at making sense of the world around them means that within minutes of their arrival they are noticing events and forming hypotheses about cause and effect. In the early months of life, they are busy learning about mathematics as part of the explorations necessary to the process of becoming members of the community in which they live.

They learn about quantity – eagerly wanting an object, then wanting one for each hand, then realizing that they have no more hands and having to make decisions about which object to give up in favour of something new. In time, they will have to decide whether they would like two or three pieces of carrot and to understand that if sweets are on offer a different answer might be preferable. They will come to know what it means when told that they will have only two more songs before bedtime. This understanding will grow alongside the experiences which make the words a reality. Young babies are rarely taught to count in any deliberate way but the concept grows as they listen to the tune of the language around them, hear the words and come to understand their significance. As the carer attempts to calm and dress the wriggling infant her words 'one sock, two socks, one shoe, two shoes' will echo their playful sharing of 'one step, two step – tickling under there'. Counting the stairs as part of the bedtime ritual of a reluctant toddler is reinforced by and reinforces the singing of 'One, two, three, four, five / Once I caught a fish alive . . .'.

Babies of just a few days old have a surprising ability (Macnamara 1996) which is known as subitizing. They can recognize a group of up to three objects, showing surprise when objects are added or taken away from the group. Karmiloff-Smith (1994: 173) comments on this ability, quoting from a mother's observation of her 5-month-old daughter:

Sometimes we play games after she's finished eating in the high chair. She loves one where I take a few of her toys, hide them under the table top shouting 'all gone' and then making them pop up again just after. She squeals with delight. I once dropped one of the three toys we were playing with by mistake, and I could swear she looked a bit puzzled when I put only two toys back on her table.

Doman and Doman (1994) claim that children can be trained from birth to instantly recognize large groups of spots, in twenties, forties or even seventies. Few parents in Britain appear to have taken up their suggestions.) More mainstream but equally surprising is the notion that babies under 6 months can match two or three drumbeats to the same number of objects and that they register surprise when simple operations on groups of up to three objects (adding and subtracting Mickey Mouse toys) do not result in the correct number (Karmiloff-Smith 1994).

They learn about time and pattern as the rhythm of their days unfolds, as carers move rhythmically and sing with them, and as the cycle of day and night becomes understood. (As many tired parents of babies who choose not to sleep at night can testify – some babies adjust to this pattern more readily than others.) The use of rhymes and songs plays a strong part in this growing understanding. Children as young as 5 or 6 months have considerable ability to predict timing and to maintain the rhythmic patterns found in traditional songs used with babies around the world (Papousek and Papousek 1987; Trevarthen 1990).

From their earliest days, straining to touch objects well beyond their reach or simply to grasp their own toes, babies are learning about distance. Their enormous efforts to move towards an object placed just out of their reach as they learn to crawl, grunting with frustration, show us the immense power of their drive to learn. As they start to move around on their feet, their first steps are supported as they estimate the distance between pieces of furniture, gauging whether or not they can get from chair to sofa without falling. Once upright, understanding of distance is further explored as babies use trucks and trikes, frequently crashing into doorways and scraping past the toes of others. With support and experience, toddlers can develop a good sense of distance.

Exploration of size and shape occurs when babies are given a variety of toys and household objects to play with. Selleck (1997: 15) gives a moving description of 7-month-old Samson's exploration of shape. She describes how he chooses to play with wheels – rolling a truck and twirling the dials on an activity centre. He watches older children playing on wheeled toys. Placed in his cot for a nap, he

> twizzles himself around the cot using his toes as levers and turns himself round like a wheel . . . using the power of his legs for spokes and his curling ratchet toes to grip the cot bars. Round and round, his eyes wide open, he takes in the dizzy, different perspectives of the kaleidoscope room . . . Samson is being a circle, a sensational embodiment of round and round . . .

The particular importance of Dorothy Selleck's observations of Samson is in giving status to what she terms 'Baby Art'. In relation to very young children's mathematical development, Samson's activity is most usefully viewed as an exploration and representation of his understanding of roundness. Art, like other modes of representation, is a thinking tool (Edwards and Forman 1993; Egan 1988) and as such supports and develops all thinking, including mathematical thought. At this stage of their lives, children's thought is primarily physical – described as 'enactive' by Bruner and 'sensorimotor' by Piaget. Toddlers' representations are rarely symbols made with markers but are more usually physical imitations of the concept being explored. If they have access to markers or paint, their representations will reflect the physical aspects of the object being represented. This is helpfully illustrated by Gardner's (1993: 75) description of a child in the early stages of developing symbolic representation who, when asked to draw a truck, will

> clutch the marker, hunch over the paper, and murmur, 'Vroom, vroom' as he passes the marker across the paper. Rather than creating a graphic equivalent of the truck, he instead converts the depicting moment into an enactment of the process of driving a truck along the road.

The chosen movements are likely to reflect the child's currently preferred style of physical action. In these early stages, this may be based on vertical lines, horizontal lines, or round and round scribbles (Athey 1990).

In emphasizing the importance of such 'ordinary and exceptional sensations', Dorothy Selleck advocates that babies are given the experiences that they need as the basis for their development as artists. The same sensations and experiences will, as Samson shows us, provide the material they will need to develop as thinkers and as mathematicians:

> All of us who care for and educate babies need to offer them the plural environments of toys in baby rooms *and* leafy mulchy gardens, meandering journeys, bustling markets, bubbling pools and all the places we visit and the people we meet . . . Babies need not be cloistered in warm plastic, swaddled in jingle music, or over protected in sterile fluffy, cuddly, cloying sweetness. A baby who is carried with us, maybe on our back with a wrapper, through household chores, out and about, will have the sensual experiences of the rhythms, sights, sounds and smells of their culture and communities to draw on . . .
> (Selleck 1997: 18)

Adults, both parents and carers, will support this early thinking and experience with language – providing labels and commentaries to enrich the ways in which very young children are beginning to understand the mathematical world around them. 'Up and down, up and down' accompanies the swinging movements that are part of adults' play with babies.

'Just one more button . . . and then you can get down' holds their attention as we finish dressing them. But some of the language comes from rhymes and songs, books and stories. These give young children a store of verbal ideas on which they can draw as their thinking develops. The words in isolation are often not fully comprehensible to the infant but within the context of interaction between adult and child they create sensations of belonging, communicating, anticipating, predicting and enjoying which will form the basis of all future learning.

Mathematical thinking from 3 to 5 years of age

The competence which babies and toddlers build up in their first 3 years of life continue to be developed throughout early childhood (and in some areas throughout life). The experiences on which their learning was based continue to be important, but over time some more overtly mathematical experiences will be added. A study in New Zealand (Young-Loveridge 1989) shows that children who do best at mathematics on entry to school usually come from families where number has a clear and visible focus in their day-to-day lives. Their mothers are likely to feel comfortable using a calculator, calendars are referred to, times and dates discussed. Conversely, there is evidence (Munn and Schaffer 1993) that children of this age do not naturally focus on number but will do so if the adults around them encourage them to do so. It appears, therefore, that young children's future ability to think mathematically, like other aspects of their development, depends heavily on the experiences, social interactions and accompanying language that children meet in these formative years.

At this stage, children's attempts to represent their growing mathematical understanding may involve symbols, which will generally be based on a mixture of their own invented symbols and those that they have seen reflected in the culture around them. Some show at this early stage that they can differentiate between numbers and letters, even though they may not be sure which label to attach to them. If you watch young children busily filling in forms in banks and post offices, even quite young children often put letters in the writing spaces and numbers in the boxes intended for figures.

Martin Hughes (1986a) has highlighted the ability of young children to create symbols to help them remember numbers. His work shows clearly that children can represent small numbers in ways which they can remember if given meaningful situations. They can also represent zero – a concept which came relatively late to the field of human mathematical thinking.

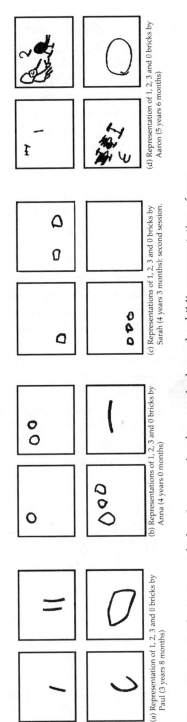

(a) Representation of 1, 2, 3 and 0 bricks by Paul (3 years 8 months)

(b) Representations of 1, 2, 3 and 0 bricks by Anna (4 years 0 months)

(c) Representations of 1, 2, 3 and 0 bricks by Sarah (4 years 3 months): second session.

(d) Representation of 1, 2, 3 and 0 bricks by Aaron (5 years 6 months)

Figure 1.1. (a–d) The bottom right-hand corner of each example shows the child's representation of zero.

Children's drawings at this stage of development show the beginnings of awareness of mathematical relationships, although sizes and quantities often reflect their personal and very subjective ideas. In drawing their families, for example, the size of each member of the group chosen by children of this age often reflects the pecking order identified by them, with themselves frequently larger than all others.

A spider drawn by John had many legs; although he knew that spiders have eight legs, his representation reflected the importance to him of the large number of legs which spiders have – the large quantity was for him more important than the specific number of legs.

Gradually these approximations give way to a more precise awareness of numerical quantities. Around the age of 4, children begin to want to count everything. Gardner (1993: 76) describes children at this stage of development as 'looking everywhere for evidence of numbers' counting the notes in a song, the buttons in their drawings of people and the letters on cornflake labels. David, approaching 4 years of age, while enjoying his bath, wanted to know how many bristles were on the nail brush. His mother replied that there were too many to count but if she really needed to know she could work it out by counting how many bristles there were in each cluster and by counting how many clusters of bristles there were. She further explained that she would then have to say that she had, for example, 136 lots of eight bristles. It was a fair assumption that this explanation had gone way over David's head – but no, over the next few days she was surprised to find him grouping his small cars, animals and blocks and saying 'Oh look! I've got six lots of two. I've got three lots of three' – delighted with the idea of clustering numbers.

Although interested in counting, young children are often still puzzling over the significance of numbers. Four-year-old Devon dictated a caption

Figure 1.2   When Victor (3 years) drew his family, he drew himself larger than his parents.

mummy　　　　daddy　　　　　　me

Figure 1.3　Julie (4 years 3 months) showed her good powers of observation and recognition of the relative sizes of things and people.

for his drawing, following the visit to the nursery of a police officer. The caption stated that 'the policeman had numbers on his shirt so anyone could phone him'.

Counting demands a wide range of abilities, not all of which develop at the same time. Sometimes young children do not have ready knowledge of number names – a 3-year-old complaining to her nursery teacher about the unfair distribution of cars in the group where she was playing, held up three fingers and said 'Jane's got this many!'. Three-year-old Nick could correctly order number names and was aware that the last name given indicated the number in the group. However, in exclaiming to his dad 'It's funny you know – I've got five fingers on this hand but ten on the other!' he demonstrated a gap in his understanding, namely that when counting you must always begin again at number 1. Sarah spent many happy hours wheeling her pram around the nursery gathering up all the dolls, teddy bears and fluffy animals she could find. She would then go out into the

Figure 1.4　Four-year-old Ben, who came to school by bus, wrote the bus number on the back of his bus.

garden and spread them around on every available flat surface, before gathering them all up again. This behaviour went on over many days as Sarah explored the conservation of numbers. One-to-one correspondence is explored by children in a wide variety of ways – placing pretend cherries on pretend cakes, potato rings on fingertips, toy figures on top of piles of bricks and so on.

Similar explorations occur in relation to other aspects of mathematics. As children cram impossible amounts of clothes, dolls and dishes into bags and cases they are exploring quantity, area and weight, and, as they transport these from the role-play area to the book corner, distance. The pretend picnic which often forms an integral part of these games involves the child in unpacking and repacking, discovering what many of us find when we go on holiday – that apparently inanimate objects do appear to grow!

The work of Martin Hughes (1986a) has been very influential in alerting those who work with young children to their immense capacity for understanding and working with numbers. He underlines their abilities to carry out simple addition and subtraction using a range of strategies including their fingers. He shows that they can invent and recall their own systems of written number notation. They can learn to make use of magnetic numbers and, over time, addition and subtraction symbols. They can use computer-driven robots. According to Hughes (1986a: 168):

> they do not confuse number with length, or fail to understand one-to-one correspondence, or believe that addition and subtraction do not alter numerosity. Rather, within their limits, they appear to be competent users of number.

He illustrates the limitations of young children's mathematical understanding, quoting the words of a number of 4-year-olds. The following conversations between Ram (aged 4 years 7 months) and Patrick (aged 4 years 1 month) and Martin Hughes are drawn from his research:

MH: What is three and one more? How many is three and one more?
Ram: Three and what? One what? Letter? I mean number? . . .
MH: How many is three and one more?
Ram: One more what?
MH: Just one more, you know?
Ram: (disgruntled) I *don't* know.

MH: How many is two *elephants* and one more?
Patrick: Three.
MH: How many is two *giraffes* and one more?
Patrick: Three.
MH: So how many is *two* and one more?
Patrick: Six?

(Hughes 1986a: 45, 48)

What is clear is that if we offer children things to think about they can create images of unseen quantities. Patrick has no real elephants to count on a one-to-one basis – concrete thought depends not always on tangible materials but on ideas which make common or 'human' (Donaldson 1976) sense to children. Hughes (1986a) further suggests that young children's computational abilities are generally limited to small numbers. They do, however, enjoy large numbers and have some understanding of their relative values. Four-year-old Sean was playing with a calculator. He filled the digital display with strings of numbers, asking a student to read what he had written. He showed great enjoyment in being able to create 99 million. Gifford (1995: 105) writes of 3-year-olds one of whom told his teacher that 'a million is more than a thousand' and the other of whom (ibid.: 111), in looking at a calendar, successfully 'predicted the pattern 31 to 41 and 51,

and [then] . . . wrote 55'. A girl watching wrote 505 (fifty-five), demonstrating some good though incomplete understanding.

Children's mathematical development does not progress in straight
lines. It is often when children appear to have made a breakthrough in
thinking that they suddenly revert to earlier understandings. This may be
because they need the reassurance of more tangible, less abstract support
for their thinking. In an incident described in *Wally's Stories* (Paley 1981), a
group of pre-schoolers seek to measure two mats, dismissing the reliability
of rulers and tape measures in favour of the length of classmates. Paley
(1981: 14) writes:

> Wally announces a try-out for 'rug-measurers'. He adds one child at a
> time until both rugs are covered – four children end to end on one rug
> and three on the other. Everyone is satisfied, and the play con-
> tinues . . .

However, the next day one of the rug-measurers is away and a major
debate about age and size ensues, culminating with the teacher using a
tape measure and showing them the number of inches each rug measures.
To her surprise the children appear relieved when the absent child returns
next day. She reminds them that they were able to measure the rug with
the tape measure but, as Wally replies, 'Rulers aren't really real, are they?'
(ibid.: 16). Knowing about standard measures does not guarantee that children believe in them!

In *Shoe and Meter* (Malaguzzi 1997) a similar situation is described;
although the children described are older (5 and 6 years of age) the issues
explored throw up the same concerns for those involved in supporting
young children's mathematical thinking. In a concluding section, Carla
Rinaldi (1997) writes:

> The real problem, then, is not when and how to explain or present
> standard measuring instruments to children (at what age? in what
> way?), but rather to ask how we can create the conditions that enable
> the development of divergent and creative thought; how to sustain
> the ability and the pleasure involved in comparing ideas with others
> rather than simply confronting a single idea that is presumed to be
> 'true' or 'right' . . . All this is much truer and more important the
> younger the child is.
>
> (Malaguzzi 1997: 103)

Stories, books, songs and rhymes continue to play an important role in this
exploration. Rehearsing number names in the right order requires a lot of
practice which rhymes and songs allow in an effortless way. Books support
children's exploration of reality and unreality in relation to mathematics in

countless ways. Young children become engrossed in perennial favourites such as *The Very Hungry Caterpillar* (Carle 1969), *Rosie's Walk* (Hutchin 1968), *The Giant Jam Sandwich* (Vernon Lord 1972) and *Jim and the Beanstalk* (Briggs 1970) as they explore quantity, size, position, time and probability. They reiterate the vital vocabulary necessary to describe quantities, patterns, shapes and amounts.

The play provision available in group settings which most children of this age attend offers opportunities for exploring aspects of mathematics, but this is by no means more valuable than the child's home experiences. At home children take part in real tasks such as cooking, shopping, tidying and sorting, in situations where they can easily question what's happening. At its best, institutional care and education will complement all that the child has learnt and experienced at home, offering both real situations and opportunities to explore similar concepts in more abstract forms. Bead-threading cannot replace the patterns involved in setting the table – one is real and one is abstract. A water tray is not better than the bath, nor jigsaw puzzles necessarily more educational than packing shopping bags.

Mathematical thinking from 5 years of age

All the ways in which children have been learning about mathematics since birth – through physical action, play and exploration of materials and events, engagement in real-life experiences, discussion, questions and stories – continue to be important from age 5. However, entry to statutory schooling brings some changes. Howard Gardner (1993: 76) suggests that 'the universal decision to begin formal schooling around the age of five to seven is no accident'. By that age, he continues, children are comfortable with representing ideas and objects through a variety of media and they are beginning to demonstrate a 'readiness to use symbols or notations themselves to refer to other symbols'. This is a major developmental step but like other developmental steps depends upon the child's experience. Gardner (1993: 76) writes:

> Of course, the extent to which such notational behaviour is engaged in will reflect in part the prevalence of notational systems in a culture. Presumably children would invent marking systems much less frequently if they had not seen adults around them indulging in such activities. Thus does culture colour symbolization as clearly as it taints every other realm of early child development . . . the impulse to create a second-order symbol system – a set of marks that itself refers to a set of marks – is a deep human inclination that will emerge with relatively little provocation.

Sadly, as Gardner and many other writers show, despite this *impulse* it is precisely at this stage that many children lose their enthusiasm for mathematics. A range of writers, researchers and practitioners (for example, Atkinson 1992; Aubrey 1994; Clemson and Clemson 1994; Gardner 1993; Macnamara 1996) share the view that it is the failure to build on children's experiences before school, to work from the concrete to the abstract, to exploit children's interests, that limits later understanding. Carr (1992: 9) writes:

> A tentative assumption for early childhood practice might be that if the mismatch between common purposes at home and common purposes at the early childhood centre is too great, or if passivity is the expectation, children will retreat into purposes where others have the power: they may perceive that the purpose is to 'keep out of trouble', 'do as the adult expects', 'avoid anxiety', rather than to take responsibility to influence the outcome, to seek a solution either to problems they have devised for themselves, or to help solve problems (as in supermarket shopping) which they know are meaningful for their community. The former option (where others have the control) provides opportunity to learn about other people and their attitudes; the latter (where children are able to take responsibility for the outcome) offers more potential for mathematical learning . . .

Those working with young children will be aware that children develop a firm understanding of mathematical (and other) concepts at different rates and in a different order. However, Gifford (1995) reminds us that the conventional reception class curriculum, with its emphasis on worksheets and colouring activities, frequently fails to tap into the knowledge and understanding that most young children already have. Their understanding of the language of measurement, position in space, selecting criteria for sorting, exploring, building and matching with shapes is often good. They show informal skills in number, such as counting, adding and subtracting, but are not usually able to represent their thinking in any formal way.

Our failure to build on what children know, albeit idiosyncratic and incomplete, often makes later learning more difficult. In later schooling the ability to 'count on' is painstakingly developed and fostered. Macnamara's (1996) research seems to indicate that it is precisely our failure to acknowledge young children's ability to recognize small groups of objects without counting them individually that contributes to the difficulty which many show in acquiring the later skill. She cites two interesting responses from school-age children. In one example, a boy who in the nursery had shown a good ability to recognize groups without counting, became distressed by being asked to do similar tests once he reached the reception class. On investigation he made it clear that it was not good enough to just say how many objects he could see – he insisted that he must count them 'saying that this was the way that they had to do it now they were in the reception class' (Macnamara 1996: 124). A further example indicates a link between 'counting on' and subitizing or recognizing groups without direct counting. Two 7-year-olds in the same study appeared to be able to recognize groups of nine or ten objects instantaneously. Asked to comment on how it was done, one said 'I always count some . . . I remember some and then I count the rest'. Macnamara (1996: 125) suggests that 'it seemed as if [he] could see some and label them with their size through subitising, and then (possibly) count on and add the rest'.

Summary

From birth children are learning about the things that humans have come to define as mathematics. To the young child they are not different than their other ways of coming to understand the world. They are learning too about the ways in which mathematics is used within their culture. They show remarkable ability to connect experiences gained from a variety of contexts in order to make increasing sense of what they have observed. An abrupt change occurs on entry to statutory schooling, when an emphasis is placed upon more formal and abstract ways of understanding and representing mathematical thought. If children are frequently presented with tasks which are unconnected with their earlier ways of knowing about mathematics, they may come to reject it and / or begin to feel that they are failing.

2

Successful learning: enjoying thinking mathematically

So few members of the general population have ever found fun or interest in mathematics, that the idea that it could possibly be enjoyable and involve playfulness and originality can be difficult to grasp. However, if the teaching and learning of mathematics are to become more effective and to have a positive, lifelong impact on children's lives, parents and early childhood educators will have to help children find in mathematics the play and creativity that is characteristic of their early development. Adults must learn to recognize and trust the mathematical learning that is occurring as the baby lurches between pieces of furniture, gauging the distances involved. The hours that young children will spend in lining up cars, putting dolls' clothes into sets, rolling and rerolling pastry scraps (which become progressively greyer) all contribute to their growing understanding. In this chapter the ingredients of successful learning will be considered, beginning with the most successful learning that any of us ever achieve, namely spoken language.

Language as a model for mathematical learning

The learning of our first language which we do as babies is useful to us throughout our lives, free from anxiety and pleasurable. In contrast, many people think of their own mathematical learning as having been tedious, stressful and irrelevant to the mathematics which they use in their day-to-day lives. Those whose role it is to support young children's learning can make use of the huge body of knowledge about language as a way of understanding and promoting mathematical development.

It would be possible to dedicate many pages of this book to an argument about whether or not mathematics is a language, but whatever the outcome of such a discussion 'the *processes* associated with subjects like mathematics, science, art and music transform them into languages of learning' (Pound and Gura 1997). Table 2.1 compares the social and cultural factors which make language learning so successful in young children with the position which is frequently taken in supporting children's mathematical development.

Atkinson (1992) talked to a group of primary school teachers who claimed that they found it difficult to approach mathematics in ways that have proved successful in children's development of their first language. They commented on their own lack of confidence, on the difficulty of working outside the school's scheme of work (whether commercial or home-grown) and on pressures from both the National Curriculum and from parents 'taught by teachers that maths is rows of sums ticked in red!' (Atkinson 1992: 10). It is not, of course, only parents who have a narrow view of what mathematics is. Atkinson's findings included the view that 'teachers are willing to try out new ideas but continue to believe that *real* maths comes out of a text book'. It is not at all surprising, then, that there are so many apocryphal stories of school-age children asking teachers who have been attempting to keep the curriculum relevant by focusing, for example, on mathematical games or discussion, 'When are we going to do our maths?'.

The playfulness that characterizes young children's language development (Papousek and Papousek 1987; Trevarthen 1990; Weir 1962) is rarely acknowledged in the learning of mathematics. Adults are less ready to regard children's apparent errors in mathematical terms as a joke than they are when the discrepancy occurs in language. Three-year-old Luke, for example, attributed the large striped umbrella which was bounding along the beach on a windy day to an elephant which had picked up the umbrella with its trunk and thrown it up in the air. His family did not for one moment think that he was mistaken. They knew that he was playing with ideas and images. If, however, he had eaten four biscuits but claimed to have eaten two, or said that they were square when they were actually round, the family's reaction, and that of professionals, is likely to have been different. They would worry that he did not have a secure grasp of numbers or shapes.

The inventiveness with which young children use the linguistic resources at their disposal is well documented (Bloom 1970; Rosen and Rosen 1973; Wells 1985). Very young children use the few words they

Table 2.1 A comparison of the learning of language and mathematics in early childhood

Effective language learning as summarized by Harrison and Pound (1996: 236)	*Current approaches to mathematical learning*
1 Early efforts are strongly encouraged.	Our instinct with spoken language is to praise young children's every effort, whether grammatically correct or not. The lack of confidence felt by the majority of the population in mathematics is reflected in the fact that mathematical efforts are less acknowledged and understood. Adults are much more likely to insist on right answers and to discourage playing about with numbers.
2 Every utterance is treated as thought it had communicative intent.	Adults take great pleasure in the fact that children are striving to communicate in spoken language. Even though adults regularly use mathematics in their everyday lives, very few are aware of the communicative potential of mathematics. It is not, therefore, surprising that they do not always identify and support it in children's utterances.
3 Learning is informal.	On entry to school, too often scant regard is paid to children's informal and home-based learning of mathematics. The use of schemes and worksheets generally discounts children's previous understanding and knowledge.
4 The rules of language use are learnt through talking and listening to others.	In our society in general there is insufficient discussion of mathematics for children to discern the rules. In societies and aspects of life where mathematics remains informal and largely unwritten, it may be more visible and explicit so that children can more clearly see how it is done, what it can do and how the rules work. Moreover, number words in some languages make the rules more obvious, such as those languages which use a form which broadly means ten-one rather than 11, ten-two for 12, etc.
5 Children hear adults all around them speaking fluently in a variety of ways and for a range of purposes.	Research from New Zealand (Young-Loveridge 1989) demonstrates that where adults do make their use of mathematics apparent and where they are confident in its use children do well in mathematics when they enter school.

Table 2.1 continued

Effective language learning as summarized by Harrison and Pound (1996: 236)	*Current approaches to mathematical learning*
6 Children explore the possibilities of making vocal sounds.	Young children (and adults) play with language and its sounds a great deal (babbling, rhymes, nonsense words, jokes and so on); fewer opportunities for playing with mathematics are generally created at home or at school. Where adults lack confidence, they are less likely to see or exploit situations where play and exploration might happen. Munn and Schaffer (1993: 76) comment that 'very few adults regard numbers as objects of play'.
7 The emphasis is on communication rather than acquiring technical skill for its own sake.	Much mathematics teaching emphasizes abstract rules for 'doing sums'. Many children fail to see what the connection is between their ability to add or subtract numbers and real-life situations. Children's informal learning can be seen as both the starting point and as a stumbling block for later learning (Nunes 1996). Adults who work with young children as they enter school must ensure that they develop the former rather than the latter.
8 Children themselves set the pace and the sequence of their own learning, within a supportive structure provided by adults.	The view of mathematics as a jigsaw rather than a ladder of knowledge, skills, concepts and attitudes (Clarke and Atkinson 1996) has not been widely understood among those who work with young children. The way in which many of those of us who work with young children were taught continues to affect the way in which we approach mathematics.

know to mean many things, including mathematical ideas. When a toddler says 'up' to mean 'I want to get up' or 'I want to get down' or 'Pick up my toy please' or 'Get the biscuit tin down please' we are delighted with their attempts to communicate and, when we can, comply with the request. Their creative use of mathematical language is not always readily understood. Kim, almost 2 years old, was nearly driven to a tantrum when she could not make her grandmother understand that when she said 'three' she meant 'a lot'. As her grandmother was tipping some raisins into a dish for her, Kim began to shout 'Three! Three!'. Hearing (and responding to) the child's sense of urgency, the adult began to put some back into the packet. After several repetitions of this operation it was only when Kim's frustration drove her to try 'More three!' that she got her wish.

Persistent concerns

Whenever or wherever we observe young children, what Athey (1990) has called their *persistent concerns* readily become apparent. Whether they are interested in trains or worms, or in the three Fs which Paley (1988) identifies as the overwhelming concerns of young children – namely fairness, fantasy and friendship – their current passions make themselves felt in a variety of ways. Persistent concerns are an effective starting point for the education of young children. For babies they are the *only* effective starting point. It is very difficult indeed to get them to shift their focus of attention from preferred objects. When babies become interested in a particular object, person or event, they effectively block out other sources of stimulation. Try as adults might to distract their attention, they continue to stare at whatever they are interested in, sometimes performing impossibly athletic movements in order to keep it in view.

As children become older and more experienced it gradually becomes more possible to attract their attention, but their enthusiasms remain important. We should not regard them as a barrier to what we want children to learn but should regard their interests as part of their task of learning how to learn. As their social awareness grows they become susceptible to the concerns and interests of the group and it is at this stage that group topics and projects (informal as well as more structured ones) hold sway in children's learning. Menmuir and Adams (1997: 34) remind us of the advantage that adults gain when they work with children's persistent concerns:

> the starting point is a challenge and a challenge is anything that confronts the learners with the need to begin asking their own questions

... it is better to start from children's 'persistent concerns' and link these to intentions for learning supplied by the adult.

Depending on their age and stage of development, children will talk about their consuming interests, draw pictures, make models, act out relevant situations from a mixture of their experience and their imagination, play with objects which represent their current enthusiasm and seek out photographs, paintings, songs, rhymes and models associated with it.

These concerns sometimes have direct and easily recognizable mathematical connections. As discussed in Chapter 1, Gardner (1993) reminds us that, at about 4 years of age, many children have a consuming interest in counting. Seymour Papert developed Logo, a computer program which even young children can use effectively to make things happen – either on the computer screen or, when connected to a small vehicle known as a turtle, with movements on the ground. Papert (1982) describes his passion for the mathematics of cogs and ratios which emerged in early childhood after visiting a mill.

Sometimes, while not solely connected to mathematics, the current concern links with something which incidentally engages the child in mathematical ideas and activities. Three-year-old Christopher, for example, was obsessed with buses. He collected pictures of buses and knew every book in the book corner which had so much as a hint of a bus in it. His drawings led to numerous discussions about bus numbers. If he was drawing a number 6 bus he wanted to be sure that people were going to get on the right one! His dramatic play included a wide range of mathematical ideas – tickets, money, numbers and the arrangement of seats are just some of the possibilities which he explored in his play.

Athey (1990) found that children's representations of their experiences (whether in play, modelling or drawing) reflected their current spatial interest or *schema* (Table 2.2) (City of Westminster n.d.: 1.12; Bruce 1987). Nutbrown (1994) discusses children with a dominating interest in *schema*, which may lead to their involvement in activities and ideas concerned with such mathematical ideas as height (dynamic vertical schema), rotation (dynamic circular schema) and capacity (containing/enveloping schemas). Whalley (1994: 96) describes 3-year-old Jacob who attended Pen Green Nursery Centre where staff plan and support children's learning through their observations of children's interests and schema. Jacob

has, according to his parents, shown an interest in string since the age of twelve months. The nursery provision includes lots of balls of string which Jacob finds fascinating. He persists in unravelling and ravelling the string and winding it between chairs and furniture and outside among the trees. He is particularly interested in *length*; how

Table 2.2

Schema	Definition	Examples
Assembling	Bringing things together in random piles or more structured arrangements	Piling toys onto an adult's lap
Transporting	Moving objects or collections of any kind from one area to another	Using a bag, truck crane, etc.
Positioning	Placing objects in a particular position – in front, behind, on top, around the edge	Lining up cars, sitting dolls in rows organizing queues
Orientation	Interest in a different view point	Hanging upside down, turning objects around and upside down
Dab	Random or systematic marks forming patterns or representing objects	In painting or drawing representing eyes, flowers, buttons, etc.
Horizontality and verticality	Exploration of horizontal and vertical lines, separately then in combination to form crosses or grids	Lines in paintings, construction, block building, climbing, throwing – swords, planes, nets
Diagonality	Interest in diagonal lines, zig zags	Ramps, slides, sloping walls, roofs, saws, serrated knives, sharks teeth
Enclosure	Forerunner of area – enclosure left empty or carefully filled in	Fences, barricades with blocks Lego – enclosing lines in painting
Enveloping/wrapping	Completely covering objects, space, themselves, wrapping things up	Putting things in bags, pockets, parcels, painting over picture, covering with blanket, cuddling
Circularity and semi-circularity	Exploring curved lines, awareness of circles then half circles	Heads, bodies, eyes, wheels Thread, rope, string
Radial	Lines radiating out from a core	Spiders, sun, fingers, hair
Rotation	Exploring things that turn	Wheels, cogs, rolling cylinders. Constructing rotating parts
Connection/separation	Fastening or joining things together Taking things apart	Train track & carriage, tying knots, staples, paper clips – drawings with linked parts
Ordering	Putting things in order	Size – largest, smallest: Number: Pattern in beads, pegs, drawings
Transforming	Interest in change in materials/life	Mixing paint etc., cooking, ice melting, clay hardening. Eggs hatching. Tadpoles – frogs
Perforation	Making holes	Cutting, nailing, sewing
Correspondence	Matching things together 1–1	Cup & saucer, knife & fork, nappy for each doll
One, two etc.	Patterns of a particular number	4 panes in each window 5 petals in each flower

far will the string stretch? He enjoys cutting different lengths of string and ties it to door handles. He is very concerned that the string must *not* touch the ground and is distressed when other children follow his string-tail and walk on it.

Whether these interests are enduring or short-lived, they provide the motivation for children's exploration and learning. They enable them to become experts and the knowledge of what it means to be a specialist can support the development of expertise in other areas. Pound and Gura (1997: 25) cite the work of Inagaki (1992) who

> describes a study involving young children who were given a goldfish each to look after for several weeks. Not only did they become experts on goldfish . . . they were also able to use this knowledge and know-how to speculate about other forms of life and as a springboard to other kinds of knowledge and skill.

Being an expert gives children familiar material with which to play and which they can think about. Expertise, moreover, gives children the opportunity to create their own analogies and to translate the ideas with which they are presented in a way which makes sense to them.

Representing and translating mathematical ideas

The work of Piaget, Bruner (1986) and Gardner (1993) has a common theme – long before children are able to think in abstract terms they will have represented their ideas in physical action (enactive or sensorimotor thinking). This form of representation can begin within hours of birth, when tiny infants struggle to mimic the facial expressions of their mother (Trevarthen 1990). The publicity materials from Reggio Emilia include a wonderful photograph of a baby in arms looking at a large shell and spreading her fingers to represent its shape.

At a later stage, their theories suggest, children will supplement these early actions by representing objects, events and ideas with a selection of materials. They will choose and organize (or sometimes literally stumble across) objects and materials to stand for other things (iconic thinking). Two-year-old Graham, for example, found a twig in the garden and rushed in to show his mother how it matched the illustration of the wolf in a favourite story of the moment, *The Three Little Pigs* (Stobbs 1968).

Emma, at 16 months old, spent long periods sorting her toys, household objects and sticks and leaves. She tore one red and one white paper napkin into tiny pieces and then became completely absorbed in sorting the shreds into piles of red or white scraps. Max, at almost 2 years of age, begins to apply this sorting activity to comparing representations, demonstrating an understanding of the link between different representational forms:

> Max has started comparing objects. If he sees a penguin on TV then he goes to his box of animals and picks out a penguin. He'll do the same with pictures. He also moves objects around and will line all his animals up on the settee and then move them all somewhere else.
>
> (Karmiloff-Smith 1994: 195)

Gradually, children find a variety of ways of representing things symbolically – through sounds (musical and verbal), colours, models, images, movement, stories and play. Written forms of symbolic representation require high levels of abstraction and are based on earlier representations.

The thinking processes adopted by young children are not the same as those adopted by adults. Through experience, development occurs which over time produces qualitative changes in the way in which children think (Bruner 1983; Gardner 1993). Bruner's idea that we all fall back on earlier stages of symbolization when confronting new or difficult ideas makes common or (to use Donaldson's term) 'human sense'. We have all, at some point when computation has let us down, reverted to moving little piles of money around in order to get our sums right.

These theories about thinking and representation are largely based on the work of Piaget, who is not without his critics. Over 20 years ago, a seminal book by Margaret Donaldson (1976) underlined the strengths but also

"Then I'll huff, and I'll puff, and I'll blow your house in." Well, he huffed, and he puffed, and he huffed and he puffed, and he puffed and he huffed: but he could *not* get the house down.

Figure 2.1   The wolf in 'The Three Little Pigs', represented by a twig by 2 year old Graham.

pointed out the limitations of his work. The strengths include the respect that his work generated for young children's minds and the way in which he opened people's eyes to the idea that young children have reasons for what they say and do.

Recent studies underline the inappropriate expectations which Piaget's work may have established in the minds of practitioners. Merttens (1996) criticizes Piaget's work as imposing a glass ceiling on children's ability to learn and understand. She suggests that the emphasis which has been given to *stages* of development has promoted an underestimation of children's ability. Far from being the 'primitive thinkers' that Merttens (1996) claims that Piaget's work led us to believe they are, young children have shown themselves capable of extraordinary powers of abstraction. She describes 5-year-olds imagining small numbers of objects and being able to perform number operations on them in their heads. These high expectations are qualified by her statement that 'children will only feel confident at this mental activity when they have actually played similar hiding games'. This view is in line with the work of Hughes (1986a) who has consistently demonstrated that, given appropriate conditions (such as the use of relatively small numbers) children are able to work effectively with abstract concepts.

Claxton recognizes the qualitative shift which occurs in children's thinking and alludes to the ever-growing range of experiences which young children face as they visit more places, enter nursery, meet new people and encounter new ideas. Claxton reminds us that we would all benefit from making use of intuition, imagination, observation, physical action, feelings and dreams. He stresses that these ways of developing learning and understanding should not be got out of the way as quickly as possible, as politicians seem to wish us to do. On the contrary they should form the bedrock of future learning, and not be overshadowed by more formal approaches. Because such approaches are found in children, we should not assume that they are childish.

Using spoken language to represent ideas

In doing so, Claxton offers a criticism of those who emphasize the importance of an early stress on oral explanations of computation. This includes both Merttens (1996) and the authors of the National Numeracy Project (1997a) framework.

An emphasis on spoken language need not cut across young children's intuitive and sensory ways of thinking. What seems vital, as Claxton (1997) himself acknowledges, is that putting ideas into words must not *supplant* but *supplement* other forms of representation. The work of early educators in Reggio Emilia offers a model. In the literature describing the exciting work there (Edwards and Forman 1993), the variety of ways of knowing are called the 'hundred languages of children'. Practitioners encourage children to make a range of representations, perhaps of the same object over time, in a variety of materials, from different perspectives and through the use of senses in unconventional ways such as drawing sounds and representing objects through sound and movement. In their view, oral language is seen as yet another representational form.

The work of Mithen (1996) offers further support for emphasizing the role of oral language. It is speech which from our earliest days gives us the ability to move between different ways of knowing – to shift between thinking intuitively and thinking logically; to connect ideas learnt at a parent's knee to those learnt in other situations. Early humans could communicate, make tools and interpret information about their natural worlds such as recognizing hoof prints. Mithen suggests that these skills were compartmentalized within specific areas of the brain. Only as we developed language did we become able to transfer knowledge and understanding from one area of expertise to another. Language made humans more aware of their abilities.

Around the world, non-literate societies use story, song and rhyme to help them think (Egan 1988). Since little children are almost by definition non-literate, the importance of these verbal ways of knowing should not be overlooked. Talking, discussing, explaining, singing, chanting and reciting play a part in establishing children's knowledge and understanding. In addition, story, song and rhyme contain two further elements which make them vital in young children's development. All provide an opportunity to explore rhythm and narrative through physical movement. Rhythm promotes dance while drama encourages physical play (Duffy 1998).

Using and translating a variety of symbolic languages

Young children will understand and use conventional symbol systems more effectively when they know how these connect with their own ways of representing things. The Froebel Blockplay Research Group (Gura 1992: 90) gives an example of a child's invented symbolic representation being used, with the help of his nursery teacher, to help him think mathematically. Edward's teacher has reminded him that he will have to clear away the blocks in 5 minutes.

(*Edward appears to ignore this and carries on selecting blocks. Seconds later, he appears in front of his teacher.*)
Edward: How many minutes was that? Five?
(*He has five narrow cylinders gathered to his chest.*)
　　　These are your minutes, right?
(*He places them in a line, counting as he puts each one down.*)
　　　One, two, three, four, five.
Teacher: . . . D'you want me to take one away every time a minute is used up?
Edward: Yes. Let me see your watch.
(*The teacher indicates the minute hand. Together they watch the passing of one minute. As the hand sweeps past the twelve, Edward jumps and punches the air with a fist.*
　　　Yeah! *he shouts, before laying flat one of his cylinders.*)
　　　1–2–3–4 minutes to go, everyone!
(*He counts his remaining 'minutes' and continues marking time in this way, subtracting a block for each minute as it passes and counting the remainder, until all the cylinders are flat. He becomes so absorbed with his tally he completely forgets the object of the exercise. . .*)

Thumpston (1994: 114) also reminds us of the importance of what Hughes (1986a) has termed *translation* between different representations if children are to be successful in thinking about mathematics. She writes:

The concept of 'translation' provides an important way of thinking about mathematical understanding. The ability to translate fluently between different modes of representation is of paramount importance, yet it is the source of many difficulties which children have with mathematical problems . . . Children need help to form links between formal and concrete understanding, building on their informal methods of calculation and their invented symbolism in order to develop, understand and use more powerful formal modes of representation.

The more powerful formal modes of representation to which she refers are second-order symbolizations, such as writing and numbers. These symbols representing symbols must be based on a firm foundation of children's own invented symbols. Egan (1988: 212) emphasizes the importance of encouraging children to see the connections between the ways in which they represent their own ideas and the ways in which other people choose to do so. He writes that 'while we are encouraging children to be makers and shapers of sounds and meanings we will also give them many examples of other people's shapes'. It is the process of translating between these representations that helps children to understand the world.

A reception class teacher helped children in her class to translate between different symbolic languages by simple but effective means. She put up an eye-catching display about their trip to the park. A significant part of the display was taken up with a variety of representations of the children who had been on the visit. Play People reflecting the numbers of boys, girls and adults who had gone were supplemented by drawings, tallies and graphs (created by teacher and children in a variety of forms), written and photographic representations. Children enjoyed counting and recounting the objects and studying the representations.

Tracking Leroy during his day at nursery school revealed that he had spent time at the graphics table drawing himself and liberally sprinkling the paper with fours. He had put four straws into each of the sand pies he had made in the sand pit and four balls of dough to represent cherries on each of his dough cakes at the dough table. He had found four little speckled frogs in a book made by the teacher in the book area and all the cards depicting sets of four from a number game. It came as no surprise that he had just had his fourth birthday.

In most children's development, the steps associated with translating between different forms of representation can be rapid and almost imperceptible. For children with learning difficulties, gradual steps may need to be identified by adults to help them to understand how one thing can stand for another. From knowing that a drink is available only when they actually taste it, children with learning difficulties can be helped to understand that it is drink time when shown a cup or, by gradual stages, half a cup, a cup handle, a picture of a cup, the sign for a cup and the word for a cup. When we witness this painstaking process we are reminded of the wonderful achievement of translating and coming to understand the variety of representations that is virtually hidden in most children's development.

There is a danger that current requirements on those working with 4-, 5- and 6-year-olds to meet the demands of the desirable learning outcomes, the National Curriculum and now the National Numeracy Project will undermine young children's drive to represent experiences and ideas in a variety of ways and through a range of media, in ways which have special meaning for them. This is particularly sad when we realize that the emphasis on some of the more formal aspects of literacy and numeracy which has resulted from downward pressures has more to do with adults' perception of what is meant by the documents than with what is actually written (Edgington *et al.* 1998). The desirable learning outcomes do not *require* children under 5 to be able to record number operations formally. Pressures to accelerate children into the use of conventional notations and symbol systems may, in the short term, result in apparently rapid progress in, for example, doing simple sums but will not lead to high later achievement.

Slower ways of knowing are not always slower in the long run, as Merttens's (1996: 31) comment that 'accumulated evidence from the last century show[s] unequivocally that too early an introduction to formal arithmetic hinders children's numeracy' reminds us. Thumpston (1994: 121) also reiterates the importance of taking a long-term view of children's learning:

> Schools can train children to become skilful operators, to perform well in the short term but this does not develop the network of connections, symbolic representations and meanings which extends the power of thinking and hypothesising.

Making connections

> We have heard much about the poetry of mathematics, but very little of it has yet been sung.
>
> (Henry David Thoreau)

> Pure mathematics is, in its way, the poetry of logical ideas.
>
> (Albert Einstein)

Mathematical learning, like all other, depends upon making connections. The logic and the poetry of mathematics are rarely connected in our classrooms, yet it is precisely surprising connections of this sort which help children to learn to think creatively. The playfulness which is characteristic of creative thought is essential to human development (Blenkin 1994). Those who were the pioneers of the early childhood tradition in Britain understood that time and space were essential ingredients for children, learning through their play with materials and ideas (McMillan 1930). Their view is reitereated by Claxton (1997) who underlines the importance of taking time to create playful links, not just in early childhood but throughout life.

Children's ability to make these sorts of links needs to be fostered early in their development since this is when neural connections are being established in the brain. There is increasing evidence that if children are to realize their full potential mathematically, as well as in other areas of experience, we must ensure that they make good use of both sides of the brain. This will ensure the development of the physical and neurological links which will help them to become good problem-solvers and mathematical thinkers. Within our culture, a heavy emphasis is placed on the logical, rational, factual and analytical approaches to learning (Metz 1987) which are generally supported by the dominant hemisphere of the brain. (For most people this is the left side.) The non-dominant hemisphere guides aspects of our understanding such as spatial awareness, emotion, intuition, making connections, our ability to respond to music and to react to colour (Odam 1995). If we want children to develop both logical and poetic mathematical abilities we should from a very early stage be supporting thought in both areas of the brain. Of particular importance to early childhood educators is Odam's (1995: 13) claim that 'movement learning is the oldest and most basic learning we experience and it can enhance and modify the effectiveness of both right- and left-brain learning'. It is physical movement which enables humans to develop complex thinking in both halves of the brain. As such it is vital to the education of young children.

Merttens (1997) emphasizes the role of adults in encouraging children to make connections with their peers – to link into one another's mathematical understanding. She draws attention to 'teaching on the rug' (Merttens 1997: 14) and suggests that the interactive processes allow children to imitate and respond to the mathematical thinking of others. She concludes: 'stories and rhymes have long been a part of teachers' "rug" repertoire. It is good that maths is now seen that way as well.' Montessori (1912) also stressed the importance of helping children to link their ideas. She emphasized the value of the criticisms which children can make of one another, without the stress and anxiety which similar comments from adults would induce.

The importance of making connections has been widely emphasized. In learning language, Wells and Nicholls (1985) have emphasized the role of connecting old and new knowledge. Similarly in relation to science, Aubrey (1994) asserts that teachers must help children to link personal and scientific knowledge. Thumpston (1994: 117) draws attention to the notion of mathematics as a 'network of ideas', aspects of which are related to other areas of learning. She concludes that these connections contribute to children's all-round development.

Many of the difficulties encountered by older children in coping with the formal rules of mathematics could be prevented if teachers built upon the children's current mathematical understanding and methods of computation. If children are unable to recognize the connections between their intuitive approaches and the ways in which teachers demonstrate calculations, they are likely to feel uncomfortable with both methods and lose confidence in their ability to do mathematics (Atkinson 1992; Hughes 1986a). Carraher et al. (1991: 234) stress the need to use contexts which make 'human daily sense' to learners if they are to learn to make use of the 'richer and more powerful' mathematics which formal approaches can offer. (Wood (1991: 99), however, stresses that relevant contexts alone will not provide sufficient connections. Teachers must also help children to understand that 'the ground rules for solving everyday practical numerical problems and abstract, formal mathematical problems are different'.

Probably the most difficult and yet most important links are those between everyday and formal mathematical strategies and language. Hughes (1986a: 177) writes:

Obviously we want children to move on eventually to new and more powerful strategies, but if these are forced upon children regardless of their own methods they will not only fail to understand the new ones, but will feel ashamed and defensive about their own.

Mathematical contexts should reflect, explore and above all link with children's everyday experiences. Carraher *et al.* (1991) have studied the mathematical strategies employed by older children and adults who have not had formal schooling. Their findings support Atkinson's (1992: 52) view that

children who are shown methods of how to do calculations, partially abandon their own methods (those established on the secure home intuitive brick wall), but often do not fully understand the ones they are taught (part of the school maths wall). In other words, when they have to calculate something in a school setting, they are often secure with *neither* method.

Carraher *et al.* (1991: 234) write:

we do not dispute whether school maths routines can offer richer and more powerful alternatives to maths routines which emerge in non-school settings. The major question appears to centre on the proper pedagogical point of departure i.e. where to start. We suggest that educators should question the practice of treating mathematical systems as formal subjects from the outset and should instead seek ways of introducing these systems in contexts which allow them to be sustained by human daily sense.

Wood (1991: 99) gives a timely reminder that the role of adults includes creating a context where children can make connections between the formal and informal systems of mathematics:

Arguments, for example, about making mathematics relevant are likely to founder if they choose everyday situations and ignore the fact that the ground rules for solving everyday practical numerical problems and abstract, formal mathematical problems are different.

Pound and Gura (1997: 25) echo this view:

> those involved in early childhood education [need] to . . . understand how the intuitive and informal languages of early learning can be connected with the more formal languages or disciplines of the later years.

Thumpston (1994: 117) reminds us that adults also have an important role to play in helping children to make connections *between* disciplines:

> Mathematics is a network of ideas which are inter-related, and to concentrate unduly on one aspect of mathematics would be detrimental to the development of mathematical understanding, knowledge and skills . . . The potential contribution of mathematics to other areas of the curriculum, such as history, where census data may be analysed and represented through graphs and charts, science, which includes the use of measuring instruments, estimation, making and testing predictions, systematic recording, and design and technology, using modelling techniques such as drawings, scale models, recognising the relationships between two-dimensional representation and three-dimensional shapes, as well as the significant contribution to communication, problem-solving and reasoning skills, supports the unique place of mathematics within the curriculum. In these ways mathematics can be seen to have a valuable contribution to make to the personal, social and intellectual development of every child.

Playfulness is essential to human development (Blenkin 1994); this is especially true of young children's need to make and establish connections. The essence of creativity and innovation (both artistic and scientific) is the making of unusual or unexpected links – playful connections. Those who were the pioneers of the early childhood tradition in Britain understood that time and space were essential ingredients for playing about with ideas (McMillan 1930). Claxton (1997) underlines the importance of speculation, ruminating – in short, taking time to think and learn.

Positive dispositions

Since most people do not expect to enjoy mathematics it is difficult for them to pass on to children a positive disposition towards learning and thinking mathematically. Research into many areas of expertise (Bloom 1985) now shows us that many people who are good at things, from remembering strings of unrelated numbers to being a concert pianist, are good at those things because they spend more time doing them. If we want children to be good at mathematics we have to encourage them to enjoy it – we all find it easier to spend time on things we enjoy!

Gifford (1995: 113) reminds early childhood practitioners of the importance of developing and maintaining children's confidence if they are to be successful in mathematics. She underlines the 'need to monitor their attitudes towards maths and number from an early age, and to guard against passing negative attitudes on to the children'. She comments – as do others, including Munn and Schaffer (1993) – on the fact that early childhood educators often show less interest in developing numeracy than literacy. She suggests (Gifford 1995: 101) that this difficulty could be overcome by helping them to become more aware of and more interested in the underlying cognitive strategies which children use.

Children's disposition to mathematics is also inextricably linked to emotions and experiences. Brown (1996) reminds us that when an experience carries a powerful emotional charge it can become unconsciously attached to our mathematical knowledge. This may be positive, but when it is not it can form a barrier to learning. Walkerdine (1989) provides a comment on an area of mathematics which carries emotional overtones for many of us. She reminds us of its implications for children from different socioeconomic circumstances:

> different children will have different attitudes to money. 'Counting pennies' may have different meanings – for some a grim reality, for others a casual game of let's pretend. Using money as a metaphor for number in classrooms may be sometimes more problematic than is supposed. The paradox is that those children who understand about money precisely because lack of it is important in their family life may not find it easy, when money is invoked . . . It is ironic that this transition is likely to be smoother for those children who already have a more abstract notion of money – one which is not linked so closely in their lives to rent, food, labour and so on.

'Mathematics is for me!'

> We can influence young children's keenness to learn mathematics by making the tasks they do of interest to them . . . by showing that we really think maths is important and fun and that it is therefore good to be a person who likes mathematics.
>
> (Clemson and Clemson 1994: 19)

Fun is never a sufficient reason for including something in an educational programme, but it is none the less essential to early learning. Unless the things we want children to learn are important to them, they will not be remembered. There is another essential ingredient in developing a disposition to learn something – relevance, not only to our context but also to our self-image. Claxton (1997) points out that if information does not fit with our image of who we are, we find it more difficult to respond to it. He cites a study in which adults were asked to role-play being an airline pilot. As part of the preparation, the subjects were given an eye test. During the pretend flying session, the same test materials were used but were integrated into the simulation. Subjects showed greater visual acuity in play than in tests – demonstrating the strength of Vygotsky's (1978) claim that playful situations enable children to operate at their most skilful. As Aubrey (1994: 37) reminds us, 'drama offers people the opportunity to show they know more than they think they know'.

Play has several important functions in mathematics, as in all areas of learning. When we encourage children to play shops, to dress dolls in appropriate-sized clothing, to fill up pretend cars with gallons (or litres) of make-believe petrol, we are promoting the function of play which helps children to understand the cultural role of these activities. Children's block play, their exploration through play of the relationship between different lengths of blocks, is mathematical. Similarly, play with sand, water and malleable materials can provide opportunities for children to explore mass, volume and capacity. However, we provide these activities not only in order to promote mathematical learning but also because they are rich learning contexts where children can reflect on previous experience and consolidate their current understanding.

Summary

Language offers a useful model for learning successfully. The learning of our first language remains useful throughout our lives, is pleasurable and is not associated with anxiety. Mathematical learning will be more successful if we can learn from these lessons. Learning to think relies on an ability to represent ideas in a variety of ways, beginning with physical ways of knowing. Translation and connections between different modes of representation also aid thought. Above all, young children have to be excited and stimulated in order to learn. The task of learning is easy when we *want* to understand and find out more.

3

A curriculum to promote mathematical thinking

Those who work with young children have a complex task in seeking to create and implement a curriculum which draws on the body of knowledge and insights which is known as mathematics while at the same recognizing and nurturing the learning abilities of little children. The demands of universities, the teachers of older children, employers and anxious parents can be loud and vociferous, while children's learning needs can be invisible to all but the well-informed observer. Early childhood educators have a grave responsibility to make sure that what Alexander (1997) has termed 'the imperatives of early childhood' are not lost among the noisy demands for early achievement. What looks like greater achievement in the short term may not always prove to be so in the longer term. In setting out to create a curriculum designed to promote mathematical thinking we might ask ourselves at least three questions.

- Is doing this particular activity going to be in children's long-term interests? As Lilian Katz reminds us: 'Just because they *can* does not mean they *should!*' Little children can learn to do formal sums but that does not mean that they should – or that it would be in their long-term interests to do so. They can sit quietly colouring worksheets, but they may be learning that mathematics is boring! Bruce (1994: 198) comments that 'short-cuts through childhood . . . do not lead to a good future'.
- Am I teaching something which will have to be unlearnt at a later date if the child is to make further progress? It is all too easy, perhaps particularly when practitioners lack confidence in their own abilities, to

give answers that gloss over a current difficulty but which, in terms of the mathematics that children will encounter later are only at best half truths. Indeed, such responses can sometimes be completely untrue! Perhaps you can remember a primary school teacher saying to you 'Five take away seven – you can't do that'. But of course you can! Negative numbers, bank statements and time all rely on being able to do so! It is clear that we quite often take away seven when we only had five to spare.

Similarly Thumpston (1994: 111) reminds teachers of her concern about 'successful short-term outcomes at the expense of true mathematics education'. In order to count we must learn by heart, inside out and back to front, the names of all the numbers. The process we use for this is a short-term one, sometimes called an *instrumental* schema (Clemson and Clemson 1994: 18, citing Skemp): we learn by habit – through saying the names, over and over again. However, if we must also learn to reflect on or think about our learning (*relational* schemas) if it is to have long-term value. Of course, children must develop both kinds of approach. We cannot count unless we know the counting names thoroughly. But neither can we apply mathematical knowledge unless we *think*. If educators give weight only to instrumental approaches, children will lose both confidence in their ability to operate at a more reflective level and recognition of the need to do so.

- Am I failing to teach aspects of the subject which children will need to support their understanding in the long-term? In considering the content of a curriculum designed to promote mathematical thinking in young children, the body of knowledge considered appropriate must be interwoven with elements which will lead to successful learning in the future. Claxton (1997: 215) calls these the *content curriculum* and the *learning curriculum*. The latter, he says, teaches

about learning itself: what it is; how to do it; what counts as effective or appropriate ways to learn; what [children] . . . are like as learners; what they are good at and what they are not . . . The learning society requires . . . an educational system which equips all young people – not just the academically inclined – to deal with uncertainty.

Guha (1987: 78–9) echoes this. She argues:

We do not know what the knowledge is, and the skills are, that the children of today will most need in the future. Flexibility, confidence and the ability to think for oneself – these are the attributes one hopes will not let them down. [Since] play is conducive to the development of these, we had better have it in school.

If children are not encouraged to think for themselves, to make choices and decisions, to reflect, to tolerate uncertainty from a very early age, their ability to do so at a later stage will be hampered. These are things which have to be learnt – they are best learnt by being nourished rather than censored. In the light of recent, extensive studies of the brain (Claxton 1997; Greenfield 1996), it seems clear that a broad early experience in relation to the content curriculum will, in opening up channels of thought, aid future learning. In ensuring that children's awareness of the world of mathematics around them is aroused early, adults can help to keep active in their brains the possibilities of all that mathematics entails. Greenfield (1996: 75) states that 'well-used connections [in the brain] encourage further development and sophistication . . . Seldom-used links soon fade.' Play, with its combination of repetition, trial and error and pleasure, is the means by which children make sure that the connections are kept alive and active.

The content curriculum: fields of mathematics

If the curriculum is regarded as the total experience which young children undergo, their feelings, senses, things seen and heard, smelt and tasted – in short, as everything from which they learn in the earliest years – it is clear that the notion of a content curriculum is much less important than that of a learning curriculum. Parents and carers do stress numbers and, from babies' first days, use counting as an integral part of their interaction with them. Many of the traditional and improvised rhymes and songs which are so crucial to development in the first year of life are based on counting, positional language and patterns. Everyday experiences form the basis of all future learning, and young children, not just in the first year or two, are learning all the time. As seen in Chapter 1, much of what they learn in these first months and years will contribute to their future mathematical understanding.

The desirable learning outcomes for children at the start of compulsory schooling (School Curriculum and Assessment Authority (SCAA) 1996) focus on numeracy, and the emphasis is certainly on numbers, but some of the objectives have to do with measures, shape and space, and pattern. Although they are intended to apply to 4-year-olds, they have without doubt had an impact on the curriculum offered to younger children in settings offering care and education to children under 5. Educators and carers must ensure continuity with earlier ways of knowing. In addressing the outcomes for 4-year-olds due attention must be given to ensuring that all young children's experiences remain broad and related to their enthusiasms. A narrow curriculum which does not take account of their learning since birth will not be effective.

The guidance of the National Numeracy Project (NNP) on what children should achieve by the end of the reception year in primary school includes four main areas: numbers and the number system; calculations; making sense of number problems (which includes money, time and measures); and shape and space. In its draft guide the NNP (1997a: 1) the project emphasizes numbers and defines numeracy as

> more than knowing about numbers and number operations. It includes an ability and inclination to solve numerical problems, including those involving money or measures. It also demands familiarity with the ways in which numerical information is gathered by counting and measuring, and is presented in graphs, charts and tables.

The National Curriculum (Department for Education (DfE) 1995) identifies three broad fields of mathematical achievement: the uses and application of mathematics; number and algebra; and shape, space and measures.

In this chapter, four fields are identified as important to the mathematical development of young children. These are measurement, number, shape and space, and searching for pattern and relationships. In the NNP, time and money are included along with measurement as part of the section dealing with number problems. In this chapter they are seen as bridging measurement and number. It is assumed that all aspects of work would be based on the uses and applications of the mathematics (Lewis 1996). The three strands of using and applying mathematics (DfE 1995: 22) are problem-solving, language and communication and mathematical reasoning. Lewis (1996: 16) claims that they 'shift the focus of mathematics further onto the development of mathematical thinking in the child' and that 'when children are freely playing, they are using a whole array of mathematical thinking skills'. It is mathematical thinking which links the content and learning curricula.

Measurement

Measurement is perhaps the area of mathematics in which children may draw most heavily on their everyday experiences. The measurement of length, mass, volume, capacity and even time is part of many day-to-day conversations. Conceptual understanding of different measures develops at different rates but is closely related to children's experience. Mass is commonly believed to be understood later than, for example, length, but

Salmon (1988) gives an example of a culture where mass develops early since young children have the routine task of carrying sponges up from the beach and learn early to select a load which is evenly balanced. More complex measures such as area and speed are not generally seen as essential elements of a curriculum for young children. They are, however, measures which crop up in conversation and which some children will have heard talked about – even if not in precise terms. Once again, those things which are important within the child's family and broader culture will be most readily learnt.

Number

In their dealings with little children, most adults place some stress on numbers – both ordinal (denoting position in a sequence: first, second, . . .) and cardinal (the quantity of objects in a set or group). Learning numbers by heart is vital – counting has been described as a special kind of song without end (Ginsburg 1977). Once one imagines oneself trying to recite every other word of a poem or song, or beginning somewhere in the middle, it becomes clear why it is so vital to know the order of the counting words inside out! Reciting number names in the correct order is, of course, not enough. In order to count children have also to learn that everything is only counted once, that the last number stands for the size of the set, that any similar items can be counted in the same way and that items can be counted in any order (Gelman and Gallistel 1978).

Number goes well beyond counting and involves a wide range of operations, many of which are familiar to children in their everyday lives – one more, only three more, fair shares, none left, doubling, halving and estimating. Money has particular significance and clear characteristics with the possibility of exploring exchange and the possibility of gaining five or ten brown coins in exchange for just one small silver one.

Shape and space

Although Haylock and Cockburn (1989) claim that adults are often unaware of the connections between geometry and number, the value of exploring shape and space in early childhood has long been understood. Over 150 years ago, Friedrich Froebel recognized the importance of helping young children to become aware of the interconnectedness of objects. Read (1992: 5) describes how the solid three-dimensional shapes known as Froebel's gifts were designed to give children insight into three forms:

1 Forms of life, by which a child creates objects seen in the world around him or her.
2 Forms of beauty, which are those where pattern and symmetry predominate.
3 Forms of knowledge, by which abstract mathematical statements are given physical form.

In the early years of schooling an emphasis is frequently placed on learning the names of two-dimensional shapes but this may not be the easiest starting point for young children. The physical form of three-dimensional shapes allows children to gain a better understanding of what two-dimensional shapes are since faces and sides are more easily identifiable. Two-dimensional shapes are, after all, representations of an aspect of shape. More experience with three-dimensional shapes might have avoided Dean's dilemma in the following example. Six-year-old Dean (Owen and Rousham 1997: 259) has been completing a worksheet which asks him to say how many sides and corners some two-dimensional shapes have. Corners are no problem, but for each shape he has recorded that there are two sides. His teacher questions him:

Teacher: Dean, I'm not sure this is right, is it? Do all these different shapes have two sides?
Dean: (Belligerently.) Yes.
Teacher: Well, can you get your shapes and show me the two sides?
Dean: (Returning with his set of plastic shapes.) Look, (holding triangle in one hand and using his other hand to point, he places his index finger in the centre) one . . . (turns shape over) . . . two.

Boys are more likely to have explored areas on wheeled toys and may be more adventurous in climbing. They commonly wander further from carers and are encouraged to take more physical risks. These experiences raise their spatial awareness and give them greater confidence and insight in dealing with problems relating to space and shape. There is a lesson here for all areas of mathematical learning – early experience makes a difference which it is difficult to quantify or explain but which we skip at, not our peril, but risking the life chances of the children for whom we take responsibility.

Searching for patterns and relationships

Searching for patterns and relationships is fundamental to all mathematics. Mathematics is full of patterns and is fundamentally concerned with differences and similarities. Burton (1994: 13) writes that she finds it 'impossible to think about learning or using mathematics in any other way than by patterning or by looking for relationships'. Even when the patterns and relationships are not explicitly drawn to children's attention, they themselves seek to make sense of mathematics, like all other areas of learning, by trying to identify the rules which will help them to understand. Thus Burton continues 'patterns and relationships not only describe mathematics, they also give us a way of looking at children's learning of mathematics'.

Athey (1990: 41) talks about seriation (which she describes as being about seeing differences between things) and classification (described as seeing similarities). She writes:

Seriation and classification have their origin in early actions applied to a wide range of objects and, later, to events. The common-sense world contains sufficient information to feed seriation structures such as size, height, weight, strength, temperature, porosity, number and so on.

Pattern is an aspect of the mathematics curriculum which is frequently under-represented in the early years. The desirable learning outcomes for 4- and 5-year-olds include a single sentence which states that 'they recognize and recreate patterns'. This simple statement masks a complexity which exists in an aspect of mathematics which offers fertile ground for the development of wonder and excitement as children explore the patterns and relationships which exist within number, shape and space. Too often, the exploration of pattern with young children in nurseries, reception classes and playgroups is too narrowly confined to activities such as bead-threading. Much is made in the relevant mathematical development literature of the difficulties which young children have in recognizing and copying patterns. In her systematic and accessible study Montague-Smith (1997), for example, draws attention to the difficulties demonstrated by young children in copying bead patterns, demonstrated in the work of Piaget. Although from about the age of 2 they are able to assemble the necessary components of a pattern, they apparently still have difficulty in reproducing it right through to 4 or 5 years of age.

To accept this interpretation is to ignore the rich potential of children's day-to-day lives and the wide variety of situations in which patterns exist. At a very early stage, babies are attracted by patterns – particularly those that have similarities with the human face. Even the youngest babies can quickly establish an understanding of the relationship between the sound of a spoon on a dish and being fed. Over time they can develop a keen understanding of the relationship between events – just try missing parts of a well-loved story! Cumulative stories, songs and rhymes with a repeating pattern are readily recalled by young children.

The apparent discrepancy between Piaget's finding and children's obvious abilities may be accounted for by the relevance of the activities. Bead patterns do not match up with the *enthusiasms* of children of this age. If we really want to know about and foster young children's understanding of pattern and relationships we should look to the patterns of the day, week and year, in music, stories, house numbers and so on.

There is a controversy about the extent to which sorting and matching are a legitimate element of an early childhood curriculum for mathematics. A number of writers (Merttens 1996; Womack 1993; Young-Loveridge 1987) suggest that sorting, ordering and matching are seen as a preparation for learning things that young children can already do. All too often sorting and matching are presented in reception classes as isolated activities, unrelated to anything else. They are seen as necessary precursors to the 'real' mathematics which will come later. Merttens (1996: 20) quotes the following conversation between a parent and child:

P: What did you do today?
C: Well I spent a long time sorting out Mrs. Williams' animals, but when I finished she tipped them all back in a box.

The National Curriculum programme of study for mathematics at Key Stage 1 (DfE 1995) does include sorting and classifying, but not as a precursor to number. Sorting, matching, ordering, comparing, predicting, sequencing and repeating can all be more helpfully seen as part of the search for patterns and relationships which is fundamental to mathematical thought at every level.

As Merttens (1996: 22) reminds us, 'mathematics is primarily an activity of the mind, closely bound up with the social context in which it takes place'. Young children are most likely to be able to recognize pattern, differences and similarities in the things with which they are most concerned and interested. That, as with everything else, must be the starting point. Educators working with young children must ensure that it is.

The learning curriculum: mathematical processes

The younger the child, the more the processes of mathematical learning resemble the processes of all other learning. The idea of any subject focus for babies, for example, is probably laughable and yet there are things which they must learn from the earliest moments in order to become thinking mathematicians. Confidence, independence, risk-taking (essential in estimating and approximating), learning from others and learning from exploration will support their mathematical development, but will also support later learning in other areas of experience, subjects and disciplines. In Table 3.1 some of the learning processes identified in the desirable learning outcomes (SCAA 1996), the National Curriculum programmes of study for mathematics at Key Stage 1 (DfE 1995) and the NNP (1997) draft guidance for reception classes are compared. Few of the learning processes are specific to learning mathematics, and the few that are, such as using mathematical language, will be most appropriately tackled when children have had opportunities to practise in contexts which are not specifically mathematical.

The learning curriculum should focus on **all** the processes which children will need in order to become mathematicians. Table 3.2 shows how mathematical learning does not only occur in specifically designed mathematical activities. (This will be explored further in Chapter 4.) It shows the relationship between 'the desirable outcomes' for mathematics (column 1) and those for other areas of experience. We need to bear in mind that:

• Children can learn mathematics even in activities that do not seem to be primarily mathematical.
• Children tend to make little spontaneous use of their knowledge of numbers because, as a number of writers have warned, numeracy is often given less emphasis than literacy in many homes and early years settings (Gifford 1995; Munn 1994; Rogers 1997).
• Even those aspects which appear to be most specific to mathematics, such as recognizing and using numbers up to 10, are most effectively learnt in contexts such as role play and relevant real-life events where children are actively encouraged to draw on their previous experiences.

As the table shows, children will be learning processes which may contribute to their mathematical understanding and development when they are establishing personal and social relationships, enhancing their knowledge of the world or when they are engaged in activities apparently focused on other areas of experience such as language, literature, physical and creative occupations. For example, mathematical language may be enhanced in talking about:

• experiences, thoughts and ideas (language and literacy);
• the environments, families and past and present events;
• control of movement, awareness of space and other people;
• exploration of sound, colour, texture, form and space.

In Table 3.2 the links between all six areas of experience identified in the

Table 3.1 Mathematical processes identified in three documents defining goals for young children's learning

SCAA (1996)	NNP (1997)	DfE (1995)
		Approximating
		Asking mathematical questions
		Checking
		Choosing (suitable strategies, units instruments)
		Classifying
Comparing	Comparing	Comparing
Counting	Counting reliably by 10s and 2s	Counting orally
		Collecting data
Describing		Describing (shapes and patterns)
		Developing a variety of methods
		Discussing
	Estimating	
		Explaining thinking
		Exploring patterns
		Interpreting data
		Investigating
	Knowing (some names for larger numbers)	Knowing (facts)
		Making decisions
Matching		
Ordering everyday objects	Ordering numbers	Ordering numbers
		Organizing
		Overcoming difficulties
	Predicting patterns	Predicting
	(Beginning to) read numbers	Reading numbers
	Reasoning	
	Reciting number names	
Recognizing (patterns, numbers)	Recognizing (halves)	Recognizing (simple fractions, patterns and relationships)
Recording	(Beginning to) record	Recording (decimals, patterns, negative numbers, data)
Re-creating patterns		
		Relating numerals and symbols to a range of situations
		Representing
		Responding to questions
		Selecting
Sequencing	Sequencing	
Solving practical problems		Solving numerical problems
Sorting		Sorting
		Understanding the language of number
Using (mathematical language, mathematical understanding to solve practical problems)		Using (mathematics, equipment, repeating patterns, variety of mathematical presentations)
		Writing numbers

desirable learning outcomes have been made. In the first row, general aspects (some of which are drawn directly from the desirable learning outcomes) are identified. In subsequent rows, links between more specific aspects of mathematics and other areas of experience are made. There are even more opportunities to develop mathematical understanding across the curriculum than the table suggests. Patterns, for example, do not only occur in mathematics but in personal relationships, words, the natural and made world, music, art and physical movement.

As we can see, all areas of experience offer the possibility of developing mathematical understanding. In those homes where children develop a good understanding of mathematics, numbers and mathematical concepts are given a high profile. Other carers should seek to do likewise. In the following section, three aspects of the learning process are explored – problem-solving, creating mental images and recording.

Problem-solving

> Mathematical know-how is the ability to solve problems – not merely routine problems but problems requiring some degree of independence, judgement, originality and creativity.
>
> (Pólya 1957)

Problem-solving has been characterized (Burton 1994; Thumpston 1994) as one of the core elements in the development of mathematical thinking. Yet it often tends, along with a range of other open-ended activities, to be marginalized – perhaps because of the adults' lack of confidence.

Even tiny babies show remarkable problem-solving abilities (Bower 1977). Soon after birth, in test situations, they are able to make things happen which they find rewarding (such as causing drops of milk to flow or making video images appear) by working out the sometimes complex sequence of movements necessary to operate a switching mechanism. In real-life situations they show remarkable persistence, learning over time to use a series of actions to solve a particular problem. Toddlers put a great deal of time and energy into solving problems and practise the steps involved with diligence. Adults who have helped young children to solve a problem are sometimes frustrated when the child immediately recreates the situation that they were struggling with. The grunts and squeals begin again as the child wrestles anew with the challenge they have set themselves.

Children's suggestions for solving problems tell us a great deal about their level of understanding and give us an insight into the power of their 'puzzling minds' (Tizard and Hughes 1986). The responses of 3- and 4-year-olds in a nursery school asked to suggest how best to empty the sand

Table 3.2 Links between mathematics and other areas of experience

Mathematics	Personal and social development	Language and literacy	Knowledge and understanding of the world	Physical development	Creative development
General aspects (the aspects of other areas of learning which are identified in this row underpin all mathematical work).	Children are confident, ... are able to establish effective relationships with other children and with adults. They ... are able to concentrate and persevere in their learning and to seek help where needed.	Symbolization is a basic element of both linguistic and literary activity and of mathematics.	They explore and select materials and equipment ...	They use a range of small and large equipment ... with increasing skill. Physical action is the basis of all thought.	Aesthetic and creative activities like mathematics are languages or representational systems which children may use as tools for thinking.
Children use mathematical language, such as circle, in front of, bigger than and more, to describe shape, position, size and quantity.		Children listen attentively and talk about their experiences. They use a growing vocabulary with increasing fluency to express thoughts and convey meaning to the listener.	Children talk about where they live, their environment, their families and past and present events in their own lives.	Children move confidently ... with increasing control and coordination and an awareness of space and others.	Children explore sound and colour, texture, shape, form and space in 2 and 3-D

Table 3.2 continued

Mathematics	Personal and social development	Language and literacy	Knowledge and understanding of the world	Physical development	Creative development
They recognize and recreate patterns.	*They show a range of feelings, such as wonder, joy or sorrow, in response to their experiences of the world.*	*They begin to associate sounds with patterns in rhymes, with syllables, and with words and letters.*	*They explore and recognize features of living things, objects and events in the natural and made world and look closely at similarities, differences, patterns and change.*		*Children explore sound and colour, texture, shape, form and space in 2 and 3-D.*
They are familiar with number rhymes, songs, stories, counting games and activities.	*They take turns and share fairly.*	*Children listen attentively and talk about their experiences. They listen and respond to stories, songs, nursery rhymes and poems.*			
They compare, sort, match, order, sequence and count using everyday objects.		*They make up their own stories and take part in role play with confidence.*	*They explore and recognize features of living things, objects and events in the natural and made world and look closely at similarities, differences, patterns and change.*		*Children explore sound and colour, texture, shape, form and space in 2 and 3-D.*

Table 3.2 continued

Mathematics	Personal and social development	Language and literacy	Knowledge and understanding of the world	Physical development	Creative development
They recognize and use numbers to 10 and are familiar with larger numbers from their everyday lives.		*They make up their own stories and take part in role play with confidence.*			
They begin to use their developing mathematical understanding to solve practical problems.	*They are eager to explore new learning, and show the ability to initiate ideas and to solve simple practical problems. They work as part of a group and independently. . .*		*They . . . ask questions to gain information about why things happen and how things work.*		*They show an increasing ability to use their imagination, to listen and to observe.*
Through practical activities children understand and record numbers, begin to show awareness of number operations, such as addition and subtraction, and begin to use the language involved.		*They use pictures, symbols, familiar words and letters, to communicate meaning. them.*	*They talk about their observations, sometimes recording them.*		*They use a widening range of materials, suitable tools, instruments and other resources to express ideas and to communicate their feelings.*

Note: Statements in italics are quoted from SCAA (1996).

pit (Pound *et al.* 1992) range from the relatively pedestrian 'Use a big bucket and take it to the other sand pit' to the ingenious 'Get a saucepan, make a hole in it, put a pipe in, put [it] in to other sandpit and the sand will go in the other sandpit'. Pippie comes up with the fantastic idea of putting all the sand into a chest of drawers which can then be moved along on something slippery. Her suggestion 'What about ice?' is precisely the strategy used by the Chinese to move across their country to Beijing a huge slab of marble which now forms a decorative panel in the Forbidden Palace.

The view that problem-solving requires far more than just good ideas is echoed by a number of writers. Playfulness and creativity go hand in hand, and both are essential ingredients in the problem-solving process (Malaguzzi 1993; Papousek and Papousek 1987). The thinking processes that are part of play – deciding, imagining, reasoning, predicting, planning, trying new strategies and recording – turn out to be the very ones that are required for later mathematical thinking (Lewis 1996).

Confidence is also vital. Baker (1995: 149) outlines a process developed by teachers in helping children to solve problems, and comments on their 'wholesale agreement about the way in which personal levels of confidence could be enhanced or destroyed depending on the quality of experience and activity undertaken'. The confidence to which Chiu *et al.* (1994) drew attention is based on what they term 'resilience'. Learners who face failure with equanimity, who know that they can keep trying and who do not hold too fixed a view of their own potential, are more likely to persevere. Interestingly she identifies 'bright girls' – good at getting right answers – as the least resilient learners.

Claxton (1997: 214) has identified time as a vital element in the problem-solving process. He suggests that it is not really a question of *quantities* of time but rather of taking one's time. He writes:

The slow ways of knowing will not deliver their delicate produce when the mind is in a hurry. In a state of continual urgency and harassment the brain-mind's activity is condemned to follow its familiar channels. Only when it is meandering can it spread and puddle, gently finding out such fissures and runnels as may exist.

Creating mental images

The seminal work of Martin Hughes (1986a) reminds us that children do not need actual objects to count – with small numbers, quite young children can imagine them. We do not actually have to present them with two elephants and three more elephants, they can see them in their heads. Williams (1996) reminds us that numberlines (both washing lines with numbers to peg on and strips up to 10 or even 100) and hundred squares provide important images from which children can work – initially by actually touching each number, then gradually being able to summon up helpful mental images. We might also take Williams's advice and encourage children to draw or otherwise represent their mental images. Fingers, abacuses and structural apparatus can all play a role in supporting the development of mental images, particularly as they provide a physical dimension to memory (Brown 1996; Gifford 1995; Tacon and Atkinson 1997).

Asking children about the images they see when presented with mathematical ideas can promote mathematical thinking. Even if they do not respond, the question may well trigger thinking which will make their own thinking more transparent to them – children will begin to become aware of their own thinking. Giving praise for explaining methods and emphasizing the variety of methods can encourage children to develop mental strategies. Williams (1996: 38) writes:

> Asking a four-year-old 'How did you work that out?', the reply is often of the kind: 'I just did it'. Perhaps a detailed answer is not necessary: it is enough that we draw their attention to the process of them doing something in their heads.

The specialist use of language can sometimes create unhelpful mental images. The use of language in mathematics does not always correspond to the use made of it in everyday contexts. What does a 5- or 6-year-old conjure up when a teacher talks about 'taking away'? It is unlikely to be subtraction – more likely pizza or chow mein. The language which we use shapes children's thinking and the strategies they choose to use. Specific terms such as 'more' and 'less' may pose difficulties for some children. Walkerdine (1989: 53) gives examples of 4-year-old girls using 'more' in their day-to-day conversation:

> C: I want some more.
> M: No, you can't have any more, Em.
> C: Yes! Only one biscuit.
> M: No.
> C: Half a biscuit?
> M: No.
> C: A little of a biscuit?
> M: No.
> C: A whole biscuit?
> M: No.
>
> C: Has [sic] you still got some more?
> M: Hmm?

C: Have you still got some more?

M: Just enough for today and get some more tomorrow.

Walkerdine's point is that children have little difficulty with understanding 'more' but for them the opposite is not 'less' but 'no more' or 'not as much'. Certainly if a young child does not want carrots, she is rarely in the business of asking for a smaller portion, or less – she is generally clamouring for none at all or, as a last resort, just one.

Introducing the formal language of mathematics in informal or play situations can help children to use and understand the appropriate language at a later stage (Aubrey 1994). If adults use specific mathematical language when talking to children who are playing in the sand or water the vocabulary becomes familiar. Further use of the same words and phrases in imaginative play situations or informal conversation promotes children's understanding of the concepts in question. As play allows children to rehearse aspects of learning, so this informal use of formal language helps children to feel at home with what may otherwise be threatening.

As with other aspects of mathematical development, the starting point must always be the child's current understanding – our efforts must go into helping each child to make the connections which will promote their idiosyncratic personal understanding. The developmentally appropriate curriculum which emerges when we work from children's starting point is most likely to promote their individual understanding. Respect for children's efforts to make sense of the world will in turn help adults to make sense of children's learning needs. The wider the child's experience of using language in a range of contexts and registers, the more likely he or she is to understand the specific use of language for mathematics. A developmentally appropriate curriculum will ensure that children are helped to make links between the languages with which they feel comfortable in communication and the formal language of mathematics. Pimm's (1981) phrase 'listen with an open ear for what your children are trying to say' is an invaluable reminder to all who work with young children. The language we use may be getting in the way of understanding – but it can be used to help children clarify their thinking. Children's use of language may cloud their meaning, but if we listen respectfully, with the expectation that they have worthwhile things to say, then their words can help us to understand their meanings. This in turn can help them to clarify their own thinking.

Children's recording

Recording is useful in promoting thinking. Sensitively used, it can help children to develop awareness of their ways of thinking. It can help them to remember things and clarify their thinking (Atkinson and Clarke

1992b). When built on their preferred modes of representation, it can extend the tools for thinking (Egan 1988) available to them. Williams (1996: 34) discusses the uses of mathematical mark-making in ways which make human sense to young children, specifically in reception classes. She suggests encouraging children to use a symbol to identify the solution to a problem, giving the example of pricing goods in a shop. Role play is further recommended as a sound context for mathematical mark-making, helping 'children to bridge the gap between a practical activity, mathematical thinking and symbolic recording' in ways which directly draw on their experience. The inclusion of writing materials alongside activities which might generate some mathematical data might also promote recording; for example, rulers in the creative workshop, a numberline in the writing area, clipboards and rulers in the block area, calculators and calendars in the role-play area can encourage children to make mathematical recordings. She also recommends that teachers get into the habit of asking children to keep their own mathematical notes as they work. Gifford (1995) makes a similar point, citing nurseries where children are encouraged to keep scores in their games. Some will use conventional numbers, some will use tallies, drawings and some will use entirely idiosyncratic symbols. Like children's invented writing, in the early stages these notes may seem haphazard or indecipherable but over time, given encouragement, relevant situations and appropriate models, children's approximations will approach standard forms. It is also clear that they are not incomprehensible to the children who actually make the marks. The adult's role in demonstrating strategies is vital and will be discussed in Chapter 5.

As the photo taken in a nursery school (Figure 3.1) reminds us, recording can be made relevant and immediate for young children. In the photo, children are comparing the size of sunflowers to that of paper plates – comparing, observing and discussing. Children at the same school also used lengths of ribbon which they called 'pumpkin-measurers'. The length of the ribbon had been cut to the size of a pumpkin's circumference. The ribbons were used to compare with the size of other objects both live and inanimate. The children recorded directly onto the ribbon – making a mark to show the length and a drawing or symbol to record what it was they had measured. These activities sparked off an interest in both measuring and recording which was long lasting.

In the long run children's mathematical understanding will benefit immensely from the use of standard symbols. They are part of a universal language, they contain a large amount of information in a very compact form and they can give children and parents a keen sense of achievement (Atkinson and Clarke 1992a). Unfortunately, the latter benefit is sometimes

Figure 3.1   Children in a nursery school comparing and discussing size.

allowed to override the disadvantages of an inappropriately early introduction to standard notations. This often has the effect of undermining chil-
dren's confidence,  robbing them of any sense of relevance and causing
confusion. Walkerdine (1988) underlines the density of mathematical nota-
tion. If children are, at a later stage, to understand the wide range of meanings that can be read into a simple number sentence such as '3 + 4 = 7' they
will need to have experienced those meaning in a variety of concrete, verbal
and mental ways.

The work of Martin Hughes (1986a) has encouraged many teachers to
promote children's invented notations. Atkinson (1992: 83) was encouraged by his writing to try out some of his ideas in her own reception class.
In summarizing the issues which she had to confront, she writes:

I continued with all my usual teaching of standard symbols for numbers. This did not seem to cause any problems.
The children used calculators and accepted their own notations
alongside mine and the more angular ones of the calculator . . .

... this class was very alert to numbers and no one showed any fear of maths.

I used games to teach mathematical concepts and to teach the conventional signs for mathematical operations.

I felt more confident about teaching maths!

A wealth of research into the characteristics of early writing (Bissex 1980; Clay 1975; Ferreiro and Teberosky 1979; Harste *et al.* 1984) has both given teachers insight and inspired their awe at the amazing learning taking place. Gifford (1995) has expressed the hope that the work of those who have been researching early mathematical notation will be similarly inspiring. If those who are responsible for the education of our youngest children gain this sense of excitement, the importance of encouraging such exploration will be better understood. Sinclair (1988) identifies six stages of invented mathematical notation (see Table 3.3) from her study of 65 children, from 3 to 5 years of age, in two French early childhood settings. Munn (1994) identifies similar strategies from her study of 56 children in their final term of nursery.

The work of researchers like Munn (1994) and Sinclair (1988) brings to maths the sense of excitement which was felt by teachers and other practitioners, some 15 or 20 years ago, when they began to realize how much understanding had gone unnoticed in children's written and graphic work. We were reminded anew of children's truly amazing efforts to make sense of difficult symbolic languages. We must remember that young children's errors may not be careless mistakes but intelligent responses which reflect their incomplete knowledge.

Anghileri (1995: 33) has suggested a five-step sequence towards standard recording which might support practitioners in feeling confident about resisting too early an introduction to formal recording. First, she suggests that learners need to explain their thinking to others. Second, they may be encouraged to demonstrate (or represent) their mental images with objects or drawings. Third, they might be encouraged to record these ideas in written form. Then they might be offered successively short ways of recording, other than in writing, before finally moving to standard notations. It is important to bear in mind the practical experience which must accompany such a process and the role of the adult in demonstrating this kind of thinking without pressurizing the child immediately to do the same. When children are learning to talk, they listen and watch for a long time before they actually make a full contribution to the conversation. We should allow them similar opportunities to see adults and other children recording in a variety of ways.

Table 3.3 Young children's numeric notations

Sinclair's categories of notation (1988)	Example	Munn's categories of notation (1994)	Example	Comment
1 Global representation	Three balls depicted as a series of eleven hook-like symbols ى ى ى ى ى ى ى			The child is stressing the mathematical aspect of 'many'.
2 Single figure	Three balls depicted as a round shape	Hieroglyphs	⌐ 6 5 ᗯ	In both of these the child stresses an aspect which reflects their current concerns.
	Three balls depicted as a B	Pretend writing		
3 Itemized correspondence (a) iconic graphics	Three crayons depicted as ! ¦ ¦	Tally mark	\ ¦¦ ¦¦¦ ¦¦¦ ¦¦¦	Most popular style. Symbols related to the shape of the object chosen – number matches number requested.
(b) abstract graphics	Seven crayons depicted as 7V	Pictograms	ᵇ ᵒᵒ ⵕ ᵒᵛᵒ Oᵒᵒᵒ	Symbols chosen to represent the number and the accompanying objects. The number of symbols represents the number of objects requested. Children of around 5 or 6 years of age using this strategy will often self-correct.
	Four balls depicted as XIOP ƷₚE			

Table 3.3 continued

Sinclair's categories of notation (188)	Example	Munn's categories of notation (1994)	Example	Comment
4 Use of figures	Three balls is depicted as 1,2,3 *1 2 3* Five crayons is depicted as 1,2,3,4,5 *1 2 3 4 5*	Iconically used numerals	*1 1² 123 1234*	Each figure represents one object.
5 Use of cardinal numbers	Three crayons depicted as 3 *3*	Conventionally used numerals	*4 5 3 4*	The single correct cardinal number is used. If asked if they can represent it differently they will attempt to spell the number names.
6 Cardinal numbers with the name of the object	Three crayons depicted as toua creion (trois crayons) *toua Creion* Five balls depicted as 5 bal [sic] *5 bal*			At this stage responses are always numerically correct.

Relevance and continuity

The curriculum should have continuity from birth through all phases of education. Unfortunately, as we have seen, there is frequently a major discontinuity in mathematical learning as children enter the reception class. Continuity will be supported by links with the curriculum of the home and that of the primary school, but always maintaining the integrity of the approach which is appropriate to the needs of the child in question. Much of the discontinuity arises because most commercial schemes of work begin as though children had no prior knowledge of mathematics. All children have some knowledge of numbers – although what they have may not neatly correspond to what the textbooks assume. One area of knowledge which they often have is an interest in big numbers – knowing, for example, that a million is a lot is exciting. Even toddlers know about 'one more'. Hall *et al.* (1996: 49) detail a conversation between two children in a nursery class. One is using the telephone, both are enjoying big numbers:

Gail: Do you want a hundred apples?
Andrew: Yes.
Gail: (into phone) Hiya. A hundred apples.
           (pause)
Gail: (to Andrew) A hundred oranges?
Andrew: Yes.
Gail: (into phone) A hundred oranges.
           (to Andrew) A hundred pears?
Andrew: Yes.
Gail: (into phone) A hundred pears please.

Sean, whose enjoyment of 99 million was described in Chapter 1, was fascinated by the differences between 90 and 9 million, 30 and 3 million, 10 and 1 million. He spent over an hour creating the numbers on a calculator, referring to an adult from time to time to check what he had done.

Table 3.4 shows how some of the broad goals identified in *Quality in Diversity in Early Learning* (Early Childhood Education Forum (ECEF) 1998) form a firm foundation for subsequent learning, including (but going beyond) the desirable learning outcomes (SCAA 1996) and the National Curriculum (DfE 1995). The bases of all learning defined by ECEF (1998) do not cease to be important but continue to be important as a thread throughout all learning.

The learning begun at birth, reflected in ECEF (1998) is continued not just throughout early childhood but throughout life. It supports the learning indicated in the desirable outcomes, and later in the National Curriculum, but learning does not cease in any of these areas. Continuity of

Table 3.4 A firm foundation – knowledge and understanding become more subject-specific as children grow older

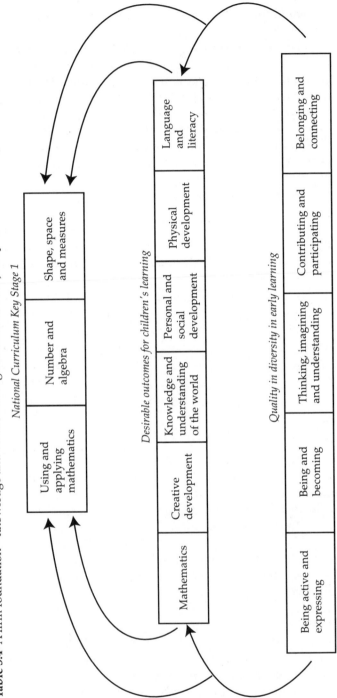

National Curriculum Key Stage 1

Using and applying mathematics	Number and algebra	Shape, space and measures

Desirable outcomes for children's learning

Mathematics	Creative development	Knowledge and understanding of the world	Personal and social development	Physical development	Language and literacy

Quality in diversity in early learning

Being active and expressing	Being and becoming	Thinking, imagining and understanding	Contributing and participating	Belonging and connecting

learning is supported when practitioners acknowledge the role of the earliest aspects of learning in later mathematical learning.

Relevance is likely to be very much dictated by each child's personal experience. This underlines the need for choice and for social interaction – these things together will make it possible for the curriculum to meet the needs of all. When giving examples or making analogies, adults need to make sure that a wide range is included so that everyone in the group can relate to what is being talked about. Relevance is also linked to pleasure for young children – we can make difficult things relevant – we just need constantly to remind ourselves how important it is to do so.

Summary

Early access to experiences which will help children to develop awareness of all fields of the content curriculum are vital in order to establish channels of thinking. The content must include measurement, shape and space, and patterns and relationships as well as number. Little of the learning curriculum is specific to mathematics, but where it is it will be most effectively learned in familiar contexts and later applied to more abstract or formal situations. In their play children learn early a number of thinking skills which are vital to the development of mathematical thinking. The thinking in action which occurs in play forms a rich foundation for the more subject-specific problem-solving, mental imaging and recording which can develop from it. Continuity in learning will be supported if adults are aware of the threads of learning – such as those identified by ECEF (1998) – which will promote mathematical thinking throughout life.

4

Implementing a curriculum for mathematical thinking

This chapter will emphasize the importance of the learning curriculum in which problem-solving and reflective thought (which includes representation) must be encouraged early and consistently built on. The ways in which young children interact with others, play and make choices will change but they will not disappear. In the same way, the need for the physical and playful ways of knowing will be complemented by other thinking processes, but will not be wholly replaced. They will remain important, not just throughout childhood but throughout life.

Playful mathematics

Child: When I play with my friends we have lots of fun . . . do lots of things . . . think about stuff . . . and . . . well . . .
Adult: Do you learn about anything?
Child: Heaps and heaps – not like sums and books and things . . . um . . . like . . . well . . . like real things!

(Moyles 1994)

Mathematics as one way of describing the world will feature in children's play. Children will encounter mathematical elements as they work to discover more about the world around them. This understanding, like other ways of describing the world, will not emerge naturally or magically but through the intervention of adults, which is discussed more fully in the next chapter. In schools and other settings for young children, it is vital not only that teaching focuses on preplanned activities such as cooking or the introduction of a new number rhyme but also that staff capitalize on responses that arise in children's play or self-initiated activity (Ofsted 1996: 18). Not all self-initiated activity is play and not all playful activity is self-initiated. Griffiths (1994: 146) puts forward five arguments for promoting mathematical learning through play. She says that play-based activity gives a purpose for learning, provides a concrete context for mathematics, allows children to take control and responsibility, provides an opportunity for pressure-free practice, and is practical rather than written. All these things are useful, but to them should be added that it involves physical action, the basis of all learning.

However, many people would say – see, for example, Fisher (1996) and Bruce (1994) – that the type of play which Griffiths is describing is not play at all but teacher-directed activity. Children need a balance of teacher-directed and self-initiated activity, which must include the time and space necessary to engage in what Bruce (1991) has termed 'free-flow play'. In many classrooms the balance is heavily tilted in the direction of teacher-initiated activities, and play is all too frequently relegated to something that happens when children have completed their work.

Moyles (1994: 3) records an observation of 7-year-old Wayne's activity in the class greengrocer's shop:

He checks the till for money, counts each set of coins, recounts the single pennies (discovering only three) and rehangs the paper bags on the hook on the wall. He calls across the classroom for a customer . . . Wayne hands his customer a bag saying 'Good morning. This shop's self-service – you can 'ave wot you wants but you 'ave to pay me.' The customer duly takes a bag, fills it with apples and hands it to Wayne. 'Them's good for ya teeth,' he suggests, adding, '6p each, that's 24p . . . please madame. Can ya give me it right 'cos I ain't got much change today!'

This contrasts sharply with the situation common in reception classrooms where children are directed to the shop and are given workcards to follow. There is a place for both kinds of activity but both are not genuine play. Only one type gives children control, exploration and the opportunity to refine and rehearse their understanding.

Games offer another playful approach. Ainley (1981: 244) suggests that

mathematical games are one way of providing the equivalent of children's books and comics; within a game there is a context for using some maths that you have learned, and that context is real for children because they can engage with it and the outcome matters to them.

There are any number of commercially produced games which can be chosen to meet specific learning objectives. However, teachers should ensure that children also have access to familiar games and can choose to play them over and over again – in much the same way as they choose favourite books. At home, 4-year-old David played a large and rather complicated board game, which had been played by the family, on his own in every spare moment of the day for several weeks. The specific learning objectives would have been hard to identify but for him were undoubtedly connected to his determination to understand rule-based games. In the process, he practised one-to-one correspondence, counting on, identifying numbers on a dice, but these skills were not his aim.

Some teachers create their own games, to complement children's current interests or the class topic. Buck (1996) describes games made in the nursery school where she works. They are linked to the school's emphasis on environmental education and designed to teach some complicated concepts. The mathematical learning in these games is incidental but none the less present in such features as using dice and developing strategic thinking.

Books and stories offer playful exploration of mathematical ideas. Margaret Meek's (1982) assertion that we define reality by exploring unreality reminds practitioners that children learn from stories. Vivian Gussin Paley's (1981) curriculum in her American kindergarten was based on story. Children's discussions in her classroom allowed them to clarify their thinking and enabled her to gain insight into it. On one occasion the children have shared the story of 'Stone Soup' and decide to boil some stones to check out whether soup could be made in this way. After an initial hour-long boiling, the children are sure that the stones are smaller. Further discussion ensues and they draw round them and boil them again. Because they remain unconvinced that the stones have not grown smaller, the teacher suggests weighing the stones. After more boiling, she suggests to them that the weight before and after is the same and that therefore the stones did not melt. But Eddie has the last word and finally adds that 'they only got a little bit smaller' (Paley 1981: 18). The language of the discussion is supported by physical action – acting out stories and boiling stones allow children to think with their bodies.

Mathematical discussion, questioning and problem-solving can also be playful. In the same book, Paley (1981: 186) describes a conversation with the class about giving change. The discussion continues over a period of several days. At some points the children agree that 'they're all the same quarters' but rapidly revert to worrying about which quarter they brought to school. The teacher herself brings a dollar to school and Eddie tells her to put her dollar in the jar, take out four quarters and put one back in – it is too big a step to put in a dollar and take out 75 cents.

Shakuntala Devi (1990: 9) describes her early love of numbers. She writes:

At three I fell in love with numbers. It was sheer ecstasy for me to do sums and get the right answers. Numbers were toys with which I could play . . . My interest grew with age. I took immense delight in working out huge problems mentally . . . there is a . . . richness to numbers: they come alive, cease to be symbols, . . . and lead the reader into a world of intellectual adventure where calculations are thrilling.

Few of us ever attain that degree of mathematical playfulness. However, Merttens's (1996: 165) story shows that when children understand that thinking plays a role in their learning they can use play to good effect. She writes:

A small child stopped me with the words 'You're the maths person, aren't you?' I confessed to being such a one. He continued 'Do you want to know something? D'you know that if you start with two and you go right on doubling eventually you get to one thousand and twenty-four!' As he said this last number, he threw his arms wide to indicate the extent and the size of this magnificent number. I expressed a suitable admiration, and he told me in an offhand manner: 'I learned that in bed!'

Even the wonder with which young children tell us simple but amazing facts such as 'D'you know? One and two make three *and* two and one make three' should remind us of the continuing need for playfulness and excitement.

Social interaction

Social interaction is at the root of all learning. Human beings have a propensity to seek out human contact, and many of our earliest contacts with babies are designed to give them a way into communicating with other humans. Conversation – with adults and with our peers, in small and large groups – is indispensable to both understanding and to the development of mathematical thinking. As a rule of thumb, the younger the child, the smaller the group within which he or she can profitably interact. School improvement studies and Ofsted documents stress the efficiency of whole-class teaching. When working with young children this poses some problems. Whole-class teaching can only be efficient if the teacher can be certain that everyone is engaging with what is being said not just by him or her but by everyone.

As adults we are able to interact with the ideas presented by one person to a group of hundreds, but even for us our thoughts are sometimes diverted by things said with which we do not agree or which we do not understand. For little children, whose thinking is rarely internalized, their ideas, misunderstandings and connections need to surface and need to be shared. This is difficult to achieve in a large group. Anyone who has ever been responsible for a primary school assembly will empathize with Samantha's story. Samantha was new to the reception class and was sitting close to the front. The headteacher was reading a story to the assembled gathering, carefully chosen to meet the needs of the youngest children. At regular intervals Samantha tried a range of strategies to attract the head-teacher's attention. She pointed, she tapped the head's shoe, she called her name and (quick to learn about rules) she even tried raising her hand. Eventually the headteacher stopped the story and asked Samantha what it was she wanted to say. As Samantha announced 'My nan's got a pink hat!', the older children collapsed into gales of laughter. It would be all too easy to interpret her behaviour as showing a lack of awareness, but it was quite the reverse. Struggling to make sense of what to her seemed incompre-hensible, the child had spotted in the corner of one page a tiny figure wear-ing a pink hat. Until she had confirmed the link she was unable to focus on the story and was therefore anxious to communicate what was for her the only point of contact.

For over 20 years (Donaldson 1976) we have known that little children do not just make sense of what they hear but are constantly trying to inter-pret events, words and actions within a context. Large groups make it difficult for children to have sufficient interaction and to ask sufficient questions for them to make sense of what is going on. This is true for all young children but especially so for those in the early stages of learning English or who have comprehension difficulties. Although the learning needs of these two groups are very different, the strategies for supporting them are similar. Opportunities to communicate ideas with the support of adults and other children, visual materials which give children some additional clues about the topic under discussion and a group size which allows children sufficient time to contribute will all help.

Fisher (1996) reminds us that different groupings have different pur-poses. She identifies four purposes of whole-class sessions, namely telling children things, imparting knowledge to them, making them enthusiastic and sharing ideas. These are all vital so long as children are at a stage where they can recognize that what is being said is addressed to them. So often, little children switch off from large-group sessions – at home and in more intimate interactions they are used to being able to check their own understanding by asking questions, asking for things to be repeated and by contributing and sharing anecdotes which help them to relate what is being said to their own understanding. With all that has been said about the difficulties of the specialist use of language in mathematics and the emphasis which needs to be placed on thinking (which for little children is frequently spoken) it is plain that large-group sessions should be used sparingly. The danger signs of fidgeting, switching off or disruptive behaviour should be heeded – they should alert adults to the fact that the situation may no longer be productive. It may even, if children are learning that maths is boring or incomprehensible, be counter-productive.

None of this means that instruction is not an important element of teaching. Parents use instruction even with very young children, but, as Tizard and Hughes (1984) and Wells (1985) show, in situations where children can initiate the topic of instruction according to their interests. It is then very effective. It is this interactive approach which is vital in supporting young children's learning and development and it is precisely this which is difficult to achieve where staffing ratios are unfavourable. Young children need the sensitive support of adults as they strive to make sense of the world, including the world of mathematics. The continuum continues to be important – 5-year-olds do not need the same support as 5-month-olds, but needs do not simply disappear.

Even though it is sometimes difficult for them, little children benefit from the challenge to their ideas which the exposure to other people's ideas brings in small-group discussion and activity. Sylva (1997: 19) reports on a study of focused literacy groups in reception classes. She writes:

> focused literacy teaching in small, same ability groups can improve children's reading ... but [in addition] each individual child spent more time engaged in collaborative learning within their groups than in talking or listening to adults.

In the same report, Sylva (1997: 20) reminds the reader of the importance of the need to maintain for under-5s 'an optimum balance between guided and self-initiated learning'. This must be achieved by recognizing that the optimum balance may be different for children of different ages, in different kinds of provision and at different stages in the dual development of dependency and interdependence. There must be genuine opportunities for children to develop the social and emotional competence necessary for them to work comfortably among their peers. Paley (1990) describes her efforts to create social networks among the children with whom she works as 'drawing invisible lines between the children's images'. She seeks to help them to connect their thoughts, to see things from the perspectives of others. The very common arguments in the play shop between 3-year-olds about whether it is the shopkeeper or the customer who pays, for example, give children new ideas to think about.

Group interaction can also help children to become aware of other possibilities. The high expectations set for one child can spur another to greater efforts. If, however, our expectations are too low or too high this may be damaging. The ability groups referred to in Sylva's report are not fixed groups but frequently changing. As teachers' assessments pinpoint children's levels of understanding in relation to specific aspects of literacy, working groups are changed to ensure that children are working with others with similar levels of competence.

Choice and flexibility

Choice is important to the development of young children for many reasons. First, if they are to become independent thinkers they need to learn to make independent decisions, alongside the many occasions in group settings where children may not act independently and where they must successfully coexist within a larger group.

Second, their persistent concerns will not always readily conform to the central themes of the classroom or of each other. Ideas may spring up which should be allowed to be followed through – to be developed into areas of expertise. If we really respect the needs of young children to represent their ideas and translate them in a variety of ways then there will need to be opportunities for many choices. Young children, whose ability to wait and to maintain an unfulfilled idea is limited, will need to be able to choose between representing their ideas in, for example, role play, paint, blocks or music. They will need to learn to select from different coloured pens and papers when representing their ideas and feelings. They will need to decide whether Lego or Mobilo will most effectively recreate their chosen image. As their control and competence grow, teachers may limit choices in order to offer additional challenges, but for the youngest children the choices (and support to explore and make decisions) generally need to be wide. Children themselves often set limits and create manageable challenges for themselves. Lewis (1996: 17) describes a group of children undertaking an investigation. She writes:

> In an activity to find and record how many different ways five multilink could be fixed together, it was the younger children in the group

who had better ideas for organising the task. They said things like, 'We won't do twists because there would be so many' or 'We'll only do shapes that can lie flat on the table.' They were setting the parameters for the investigation and also justifying every model as they went.

The third reason for emphasizing the importance of choice is related to the need for children to make connections in their learning. The nature of young children's learning is necessarily idiosyncratic. If you've only been alive for 18 or 36 or even 50 months you have little experience with which to connect. Each toddler's limited experience will have relatively few points of overlap with the experiences of other toddlers of a similar age. Their choices will reflect their own concerns and sometimes come to mirror the choices of others.

Flexibility is what we hope will develop in children, but it is also essential in adults. Regular observations of children's learning will provide adults with insights which they can assess against their priorities for the child. The curriculum map offered by documents like the National Curriculum and the desirable learning outcomes offer goals against which children's progress may also be judged. Regular evaluation of children's records will enable staff to keep in mind what they want children to learn over time and seize on opportunities that arise in children's play and through discussions with them. This will be discussed further in the next chapter.

Children can develop flexible ideas through discussion – a choice of vocabulary or strategy may be introduced, sometimes in a planned way, sometimes by chance. Merttens and Vass (1990: 25) emphasize that:

> Flexibility in language may give us flexibility in approaching a problem . . . a limited command of language may narrow the choice of strategy we take to a particular task.

Real-life experiences

Throughout this book an emphasis has been placed on the importance of linking the more abstract forms of mathematics to children's first-hand experiences. For young children real-life experiences are important not just on this basis but as continued grist to their mill. Real-life experiences are needed to extend and develop their understanding of the world in general, which is of necessity very limited. A child of statutory school age has little more than 60 months of experience. Among those entering a reception class with a single point of entry, the oldest will have 60 months of experience, while the youngest will have only 80 per cent of that. Real-life experiences like riding on a bus, visiting the market and pegging out the washing offer children the opportunity to reflect on their own experience and to compare it to the experiences of other children. For younger children in day care, they provide a chance to learn from everyday experiences which they might otherwise miss out on. Such activities are rich in mathematical potential.

Cooking provides a commonly used example. In early years setting cooking is often cited as a useful mathematical activity, and of course it is. It may include counting, weight, estimation, capacity and volume. However, it also includes a wide range of possibilities which includes small motor control, scientific concepts, the opportunity to develop vocabulary, sharing, planning and sensory experience. It will only support mathematical thinking if adults actually develop and exploit the mathematical elements. If staff are focusing on number, for example, with a group of children then recipes that focus on number may be chosen to reinforce understanding. This can be achieved through recipes that use a specific number of spoonfuls, eggs, vegetables or fruits. A similar focus on weight or halving or area may be planned.

However, if early learning is to be effective, early childhood educators must not lose sight of the possibility that children have questions that go beyond 'how much' and 'how many'. Real-life experiences have meanings which both go beyond and encompass mathematics and the other subjects, disciplines or areas of experience.

We may identify possible learning outcomes, but we must be prepared for the fact that young children's interests may lead them into alternative paths. They will not always learn what we set out to teach them. We must constantly evaluate both what they have learnt and what we hope to teach them. For example, the nursery school children had been taken to the Natural History Museum to follow up a project on mammals. On returning to school, they were asked what they had liked best. 'Going upstairs on the red bus' said Matthew!

Mathematics from 0 to 3

Good programs for children from birth to age 3 are distinctly different from all other types of programs – they are not a scaled-down version of a good program for preschool children.

(Bredekamp 1987: 17)

Throughout these years, children's development depends heavily on their interactions with adults who know them well enough to interpret their intentions. (If babies and toddlers are cared for outside the home at any point during the week, there will need to be close partnership between the parents and carers to ensure that their intentions are understood.) We are now also increasingly aware of how they benefit from interaction and contact with other children of all ages, including those close to them in age (Dunn 1988). Their focus is inevitably on making sense of their world and daily routines offer golden opportunities to help and guide them in this process.

Adults also have a vital role in modelling talk and play. Children's own play (whether solitary or alongside other children) should not be intruded upon, for it is here that they are practising, rehearsing and representing things that they have seen, heard and experienced. It is here that they are laying the foundations for thought – including mathematical thinking. However, adults can nurture this early play by playing with children in order to model the process of making one thing stand for another, pretending, sequencing and exploring. Adults also have a vital role to play in helping children to sustain play by maintaining their interest (Bredekamp 1987). Once again the importance of building on the child's own interests is underlined – how often have you seen a toddler slide away from something he had been happily engaged in when an adult moves in and asks questions? The most effective support is watchful and sensitive to what the baby wants to do, supporting rather than diverting or distracting play.

Whatever the experiences offered to young children in these crucial years, the quality of care and stimulation they experience shapes their learning opportunities and forms the basis of all future learning. The curriculum of the subsequent years of early childhood does not supplant this foundation but should be seamlessly moulded to it. The curriculum should form a continuum which will encompass the notions of:

- building on children's own interests;
- adults interacting with children's learning;
- the need for play; and
- social interaction.

Routine tasks and day-to-day activities are used to help children learn about their world and their response to it. Good-quality provision will ensure that stimulation, fun and interaction are offered within a predictable order to the day, providing a clear rhythm.

Anything and everything within the environment will be seen as play materials by children of this age, so adults have to make sure that everything within reach is safe, neither harming the child nor, if precious, susceptible to damage. The heuristic play materials developed by Goldschmied (1990) offer babies and toddlers opportunities to explore and develop their sensory understanding – which will be the basis of future conceptual development. Throughout these years solitary and parallel play will be a dominant feature of their activity and this should be both respected and catered for (Bredekamp 1987) – little children cannot happily wait for their turn. Learning to take turns will receive a greater focus later in their development. In group settings this will often mean having several of the same toys so that the current favourite can be enjoyed by more than one child.

From their earliest months babies can enjoy books (Butler 1979) – repetitive language, striking illustrations and a cosy lap may make them an enjoyable and stimulating experience. Just as the adult's prime intention in sharing books with babies is not to teach them to read, so sharing number rhymes and joining in lively games is not solely about mathematical development. The enjoyment of learning and broadening horizons in general are among the adult's foremost but often unspoken intentions.

Compare this happy scene of books, rhymes, exploration, play and physical interaction with the picture summoned up by the work of Doman and Doman (1994). Their book sets out a method by which they claim very young children can be taught to recognize large numbers of spots drawn on big cards and to undertake some quite complex sums, including equations. If their claims are true, one is left asking why; although, to be fair, they do say that if either the parent or the child is not having fun then the work should be abandoned. The same concerns about linking the abstract nature of the symbols used to children's practical understanding will apply to these babies and toddlers as apply to children in the reception class being introduced to formal mathematics for the first time. Earlier does not necessarily mean better! What is perhaps of most concern about their work is that it violates the balance of adult-directed and child-initiated activity. They recommend, for example, that parents might put their mathematics programme (which requires three short practice sessions a day) into practice from birth. With a heavy emphasis on instruction, this leaves little time for play, interaction and exploration.

Mathematics from 3 to 5

Bredekamp (1987: 48) observes that children of this age need 'large amounts of uninterrupted time indoors and outdoors'. This, she says, will allow them to learn to persevere and give them the opportunity to practise new learning. She echoes Margaret McMillan's (1930) emphasis on allowing plenty of time and space in order to enable children to develop their understanding of themselves, others and the world. This she says should be achieved 'through observation, interacting with people and real objects and seeking solutions to real problems' (Bredekamp 1987: 48).

The traditional activities found in nursery schools and classes, day nurseries and playgroups have been developed over many years to stimulate children's curiosity, to heighten their motivation to extend their learning beyond the routine tasks and materials of the home and to support their desire to understand the world around them.

The need for a safe and predictable environment remains but the balance needs to include new and shared experiences. Even familiar activities such as going shopping take on a new slant and offer a renewed learning opportunity – children are learning to see things with new eyes, to compare their experiences and to challenge one another's understanding.

A number of recent publications (Clemson and Clemson 1994; Lewis 1996; Montague-Smith 1997) have helpfully begun to identify opportunities for learning mathematics in early years settings – these are frequently open-ended and may give teachers and other workers good ideas for developing the mathematics curriculum. In the early years self-evaluation framework produced by Leeds Under Eights Service (1996: 40) the mathematics section lists a range of ideas headed:

Mathematical experiences are about . . .
   organising the cars so they all fit in the car park
   looking forward to becoming 5 years old; organising my party
   guessing how high the aeroplane is
   building a wall that the wolf can't blow down
   buying fruit to make a fruit salad
   making a tent big enough for all my friends
   sorting and putting away my toys
   printing patterns on fabric for curtains in the home corner
   wondering why the tall thin bottle holds less than the short fat
   bottle
   noting whose sunflower has grown the tallest
   planning a cafe in the role play area . . . what goes where?

This is helpful in encouraging confidence among staff as to what constitutes mathematics. Even those staff most lacking in confidence can, as they collect observations of children's responses in these kinds of activities, begin to gain insight into the breadth and depth of children's mathematical understanding.

Much less helpful are those publications which produce series of worksheets for use in nursery classes. There is no place in the nursery for worksheets. Fisher (1996) has identified some important principles to bring to mind when tempted to make use of worksheets. She reminds practitioners that worksheets do not give an accurate view of what children can do – only careful observation of what they do and say can give that insight. She underlines the fact that young children need to develop their own ways of recording their ideas. Finally, she advises teachers to think of more effective ways to address independence and self-initiated activity – worksheets are frequently used to keep children busy and seated in one place. Since the vast majority of children who have nursery places in Britain are in part-time provision, they have little enough time to play, explore and interact in group settings. Adults must not squander children's precious time by filling it with time-wasting time-fillers.

The desirable learning outcomes

The desirable learning outcomes (SCAA 1996) are being used in the inspection of early education (nursery and reception classes) as a benchmark of national attainment. This is unfortunate – the prescribed outcomes are not based on research findings. In theory they are an extrapolation of the National Curriculum. The thinking is that if we wish most children to attain level 2 by the end of year 2, by the start of year 1 they will need to be attaining level 1 (given that each level is broadly supposed to represent 2 years of development). To this complicated picture has now been added the guidance for the National Numeracy Project. Of themselves the goals stated in these documents need not be contentious. Nothing is written there that anyone would not wish young children to be doing. However, what is missing are the opportunities for the 'ecstatic responses' (Egan 1988) which drive young children to learn. What is unhelpfully present is a wording which enables those who have a narrow view of mathematics and young children's learning to interpret the outcomes as demanding formal recording at an inappropriate stage of development. The wording 'Through practical activities children understand and record numbers, begin to show awareness of number operations, such as addition and subtraction, and begin to use the language involved' (SCAA 1996: 3) does not demand that. Indeed, by referring to children *beginning* to use the language involved, it is clear to early childhood specialists that formal recording would, in preceding linguistic competence, be premature.

Mathematics in the primary school

Many children beginning school will be under 5 years of age and the approach described in the previous section will need to be maintained for them. Indeed the introduction to the desirable learning outcomes (SCAA 1996), makes it clear that where necessary it may be maintained throughout reception and into Key Stage 1. The reservations expressed by some writers about early entry to school (Sharp 1997; Joseph 1993) should be borne in mind in considering an appropriate curriculum.

Bredekamp (1987: 71), in referring to a developmentally appropriate curriculum for children over 5 suggests the following:

> The goal of the math program is to enable children to use math through exploration, discovery and solving meaningful problems. Math activities are integrated with other relevant projects, such as science and social studies. Math skills are acquired through spontaneous play, projects and situations of daily living. Teachers use the teachers' edition of the maths textbook as a guide to structure learning situations and to stimulate ideas about interesting math projects. Many math manipulatives are provided and used. Interesting board and card, paper and pencil and other kinds of games are used daily. Non-competitive, impromptu oral 'math stumper' and number games are played for practice.

This approach contrasts sharply with the approach used in many reception classes – where work does not draw on the integrated learning opportunities, and where children work through workbooks or worksheets slavishly. Where classes are large and staffing ratios unfavourable such devices may offer busy teachers valuable respite, but they do not support mathematical thinking. Children tend to be directed to work through the materials at their own pace, regardless of their understanding. This inflexible practice, common in reception and other primary classes, of moving groups of children through the same activity is commented on by Clemson and Clemson (1994: 19):

> There is no theoretical justification for processing children at different rates through the same material. Rather, depending on the interests and desires of the child, a wide range of mathematical ideas should be available to children, and in a variety of classroom created contexts.

In the 1950s and 1960s, structured materials such as Stern apparatus and Cuisenaire rods were widely used, and much of the apparatus remains in classroom cupboards. A recent study reported by Tacon and Atkinson (1997) suggests that structured apparatus can help children to create mental images and thus support their ability to solve mathematical problems mentally. It should be supplemented by ready access to numberlines and number squares. Just as classrooms have alphabets, readily available for reference, so hundred squares, displayed so that children can refer to them, stimulate many children's interest.

National Numeracy Project

The draft guidance (NNP 1997a) for children in reception classes recognizes the very different stages (and the wide spread of their relative ages) which such young children are at on entry to school. It helpfully reiterates that some children in reception classes are below statutory school age and recognizes the continuity which needs to exist between different age groups. The framework reminds practitioners that reception class provision will include role play, outdoor activities, blocks, natural materials, a graphics area and games and puzzles – all of which can usefully be exploited to support mathematical learning. It differentiates between planned, adult-directed sessions and activities which are to be developed on a more spontaneous basis. There are, however, some worrying aspects – the required daily 45-minute session which it is stated should, by the end of the reception year, involve the whole class working together does not address the differing needs of the summer-born children despite recognizing the difference in age. Forty-five minutes is a very long time to engage in 'an aural, interactive lesson with the whole class', particularly if some members of the class speak English as a second or subsequent language or if their competence in their first language is immature. Even by the end of the reception year, some children have still not attained statutory school age. Discussions with smaller groups, with a short whole-class session, are better suited to the needs and maturity of young children entering school – particularly when it is remembered that many of the children involved are barely 4 years old. The further suggestion that the session might take the form of

> an introduction with the whole class, then activities that are worked on by groups or individuals over half a day, with a plenary later in the day: for example activities with a number focus set up in the post office area, with **children taking turns to work in that area**

fails to take account of all that is known about young children's learning. Taking a turn in the post office area is not the only way to learn about mathematics. It is highly unlikely that a specific activity for the whole class, whether conducted as a whole class or not, will meet the needs of all. Choices and opportunities for decision-making can still be offered, children's enthusiasms can still be acknowledged.

The National Numeracy Project team has produced a video (NNP 1997b) which includes work in an Hungarian nursery. This is seen as offering a useful model since mathematical attainment there is among the highest in Europe. The children do not start school until they are aged 6, so the children in the nursery are the equivalent of British year 1 children. The video explains that Hungarian nursery-aged children have a largely unstructured day with long periods of play broken only by their daily structured 45-minute period of mathematical activity as a whole class. The NNP attributes Hungary's success to the structured session. An equally good hypothesis is that it is the delayed start to formal education and the long periods of play which create the foundation for later mathematical achievement.

National Curriculum

The National Curriculum (DfE 1995) has exerted a downward pressure on the curriculum for young children. However, the drive for achievement is in opposition to the repetitious and narrow tasks that many children are given to do. If challenged, teachers will often say that they have to work in particular ways because of the National Curriculum. There are aspects of the National Curriculum programmes of study for mathematics which do not sit easily with young children's learning needs, but there are many others that do. Throughout the Key Stage 1 programme of study there are both explicit and potential opportunities for children to work actively and interactively, to make decisions, reflect on and represent their ideas and to play both indoors and out. As Edgington and her colleagues show (1998), practitioners can interpret the National Curriculum in order to ensure that tasks and activities enable children to learn in effective ways which build on their current understandings.

Summary

Adults offering children a curriculum to develop their mathematical thinking need to provide choices so that children can build upon their persistent concerns. They need to ensure that children interact with others – sometimes and for relatively short periods in larger groups but most effectively in small groups. Interaction with adults is vital, but learning also occurs in situations where children are interacting with their peers. The curriculum should reflect and build upon children's real-life experiences. Above all, it should offer time and space for playful approaches to mathematical learning, which will include teacher-directed activity. This cannot replace self-initiated play, but may, through games, books, stories and discussions, offer a variety of learning opportunities.

From birth to age 3, children's learning will be best supported by an emphasis on learning and developing through everyday experiences and routines. The traditional provision of group settings for older children offers the kinds of activities which allow children to think in action, representing their growing understanding of mathematics in play, talk, movement and sound, as well as two- and three-dimensional images. The desirable learning outcomes, National Numeracy Project and National Curriculum all exert pressures which practitioners who lack confidence sometimes interpret as requirements. These should be judged in the light of all that is known about young children's learning and in that way can provide a helpful map of children's mathematical journey – to be safely stored in the practitioner's head.

5

Observing, planning and supporting mathematical thinking and learning

Extraordinary as it may appear, especially to those who believe strongly in the power of nurturing and who reject the notion that human beings are nothing more than a collection of genes, babies' prime carers generally have innate or natural knowledge of how best to support the development of their precious responsibility. In reality, just as the baby has a propensity to work at making sense of the world, to figure out the rules and to seek out human interaction, so others, including even slightly older children, have a propensity to do the things that will make that possible. Research (Papousek and Papousek 1987; Trevarthen 1990) shows us that the responses of adults to very young children are too rapid to have been consciously planned and must therefore rest on implicit understandings. Where, in research settings, the carer's responses are manipulated (through the use of video and mirrors) to be delayed or not matched to the actions of the baby, the latter shows real distress. In real-life rather than research settings, such delays may occur where the adult is not tuned in to the baby's needs. This may be because the adult is overwhelmed by pressures, possibly financial or emotional or both. It may be because his or her own experience of care as an infant is such as to evoke destructive memories which act as a barrier to good interaction with the baby. However, this is relatively rare and in general we must conclude that adults dealing with young babies in apparently unstructured settings, such as informal play in the home, do closely *observe* what their babies do and *intervene* appropriately.

The work of Wells (1985), for example, shows that in talking to their children, parents limit or structure the sentence complexity which they use to reflect children's understanding. They extend the complexity in two ways. If an adult uses a more complex structure by mistake and realizes that the child can cope with it, that will become part of the future repertoire when interacting with the child. Sentences with more than one clause are a common example of where this happens. Unusual words to which the child unexpectedly responds are another. Furthermore, if the parent hears the child use or respond to a more complex form they will again weave that into their conversations. A common example occurs in the use of 'I' and 'me'. Before children fully understand the importance of these words, adults get into very convoluted discussions with young children. Once they hear the child using them appropriately the translations which accompanied earlier conversations such as 'Give it to me, give it to mummy' become redundant. Tremendously skilful and unconsciously reflective as this process is, it works well in the home where adults are generally dealing with just one baby who is very well known to them. Overt planning is unnecessary since the adults' prime goal is simply to bring the child successfully into the world of the family – which is modelled before the child every single day.

Within institutional care, adults will generally be dealing with larger numbers of children from a range of homes and cultures whose family values and customs will differ. The adults' role is to bring the children up not only according to the will of their family but also in line with the demands of society. Again there will usually be some common threads, but there will also be differences. Professional carers will have less intimate knowledge of the children's understandings and enthusiasms and their own goals for the children will be less focused because of conflicting demands. Thus professionals can rarely act in the same 'natural' way as parents. Observing and intervening remain crucial ingredients of the success of their work with babies and young children, but to these must be added planning. Careful planning will allow parents or other principal carers to discuss with staff what their child's experiences will be. Quality assurance procedures can be used to ensure that plans do not conflict with either families' concerns or children's entitlement. Without the involvement of all parties, observation will be based on restricted information and intervention may be based on a false premise.

Observing children's mathematical learning and thinking

Everyday things hold wonderful secrets for those who know how to observe and to tell about them.

(Gianni Rodari)

One of the exciting features of early childhood education is the way in which the pioneers or founders of the tradition – including such notables as Friedrich Froebel, Maria Montessori, Margaret McMillan and Susan Isaacs – were able to tease out the learning needs of young children through their own sensitive observation. Their insights (and the importance of a developmentally appropriate curriculum) are today increasingly supported by the findings of developmental psychologists and educationalists. In relation to social contact (Dunn 1988; Trevarthen 1990; Vygotsky 1986), the role of movement in development (Athey 1990; Davies 1995) and the benefits of developing both left and right functions of the brain (Claxton 1997; Greenfield 1996), the importance of the observations of the early pioneers is underlined. The terminology may have changed, but the messages are similar.

The stories that observations tell

In Reggio Emilia, adults working with young children in the city's nurseries understand that their observations of children's learning are of fundamental importance. The detailed notes (called 'documentation') kept by practitioners are used to help staff to develop a story or theory and thus to promote understanding of children's learning. Malaguzzi (1997: 11) writes:

> Though documentation may have originated as a way to offer children an opportunity to evaluate their own work and to keep parents better informed about school experiences, it was soon discovered to be an extraordinary opportunity for teachers to revisit and re-examine their own work with children, offering unquestionable benefits in terms of professional development . . . In this light, documentation becomes an integral part of educational planning and organisation and an indispensable tool for listening, observing and evaluating . . . it is my deep conviction that the world of school must begin to understand that producing documents and testimonies to the educational experience means drawing closer to a better understanding of the workings of the human mind and of children's learning styles and strategies of behaviour.

Vivian Gussin Paley also emphasizes the importance of narrative observations in understanding children's learning. In her book entitled *The Boy Who Would Be a Helicopter* (1990: xii) she writes about Jason and about teachers making sense of the world of learning:

> None of us are to be found in sets of tasks or lists of attributes; we can be known only in the unfolding of our unique stories within the

context of everyday events. We will listen to Jason's helicopter stories and offer our own in exchange . . . The story of Jason and his helicopter reminds us that every child enters the classroom in a vehicle propelled by that child alone, at a particular pace and for a particular purpose.

Evaluating the curriculum

Regular evaluation of children's ongoing records is essential. It ensures that the potential offered by areas of the nursery or classroom for developing mathematical thinking is recognized and that the emerging needs of young learners are regularly addressed. The observations of those who work with young children have stories to tell, not only about individual development, or about human learning in general, but also about the quality and relevance of provision. Practitioners' observations can tell them a great deal about the effectiveness of what they are planning and of what they have provided for children. If areas of provision are underused, or sometimes misused, practitioners should ask themselves whether that is because curriculum planning has been insufficiently thoughtful or reactive to children's needs. If a number of children are having difficulty with a particular area of development, is it because there has been insufficient opportunity for them to engage with relevant activities and learning experiences?

A nursery team, piloting a new assessment schedule for a publisher, was surprised to find that most of the children in the class were apparently unable to sort objects by length. This was an area that they had assumed the rich provision in the nursery made children aware of. They began to observe children engaged in activities where length was a potential topic of conversation. By discussing their observations, staff realized that provision did not routinely encourage children to consider length. Over time they began to make changes. In the outside water area they added piping of all lengths – some very short, some very long. In the creative workshop area they added a large number of very long and very short cardboard tubes. Into the dressing-up clothes were placed long pieces of ribbon and material. Long and short straws were placed on the milk table. Making banana bread provided an opportunity to discuss the relative lengths of the fruit and whether to use the longer or shorter baking tins. Conversations about longer and shorter cooking times promoted further thought. Ongoing observations showed that the children, after just a week or two, were more aware of length and comparisons and used the relevant vocabulary more frequently in their informal conversations.

Evaluation should include consideration of the extent to which equality of opportunity is being maintained within the setting. Evaluation of this type goes beyond looking at individuals and should seek to analyse what has been observed in the light of the response of *groups* of children. If no boys have chosen to go to the graphics area of the classroom, or if girls have not managed to use a computer all week, that is not only an issue about individual children but also a question of provision and intervention.

Observing the learning of individual children

Besides these broader purposes for observation lies the fundamental one of observing the learning of individual children. If we are really to see children operating at their most effective, the more natural and real the context in which we observe them the better. Just as we know that children's talk (and writing) is richer and more communicative when they have real things that are important to them to discuss, so it is with mathematics. Ainley (1981: 248) writes about older children but her ideas apply equally to young children: 'If we really want to know about children's attainment in mathematics, we need to watch them doing some real mathematics; we may be surprised at what we see.' For young children, real mathematics will involve not only the games that Ainley used in her research, but also real-life activities, play and investigations. If we make time to talk to children, to observe from a distance and to participate in their activity, we will gain a range of invaluable insights. Working with young children is so demanding that adults frequently find it difficult to stand back and watch. They may often feel that they are diverted from what they plan to do by a bleeding knee or a distressed arrival. Careful planning to ensure that all adults in the team have a clear agenda can help to ensure that vital observations are made.

There are issues about when and how to observe. These should be resolved through team discussion – decisions will be based on previous observations and staff evaluation. Written plans should identify children and areas to be observed. In order to assess young children's mathematical thinking, observations will need to draw on children's physical activity and their conversations. There is absolutely no issue about *who* should observe – all who are involved with and concerned for the child, including his or her parents and other principal carers, should be encouraged to contribute their unique perspective of the child's mathematical development. There is added strength in the differing viewpoints that adults bring to the way in which they observe, which will be derived from their training and experiences.

In relation to *what* to observe it is important that we do not simply observe activities that look 'mathematical'. In too many settings for young children, planning sheets have a box marked 'maths' which each day is filled in with suggestions like 'number puzzles', 'threading beads' and 'pegboards'. Of course these activities have mathematical potential and by involving ourselves in them we may learn something of what children know about mathematics. However, listening to their talk while they are with friends on the climbing frame or riding bikes may tell us about their understanding of space and position. Davies (1995: 61) describes 3-year-old Nicola playing on an empty clothes rail in a department store. She writes:

> Nicola had established an activity around the bottom rail and one of the uprights, saying aloud this sequence to herself as she moved:
> under and over
> under and over
> under and over
> round and round and round and round

Such an observation – an everyday occurrence – tells us, if we have eyes to see and ears to hear, that Nicola has understanding of pattern (both rhythmic and linguistic) and that she can match the language and physical action of position. The better we know her the more likely we are to be able to make further hypotheses about the significance of a single observation. Gathering observations about a child's thinking and understanding can only be done effectively over time. It may be useful to think of it as somewhat like the Victorian art of *découpage* where layer is added to layer of a picture until a three-dimensional effect emerges. So it is with our observations. One observation or conversation tells us something, two observations tell us more, perhaps confirming our original view, perhaps conflicting with it. As time goes on we gather a clearer and clear view, but always with a big question mark over it. Practitioners' observational evidence should always pose new questions which may be followed up in further observations, changes in provision and direct support for groups and individuals.

Video of children's activity over a period; scrappy notes made hurriedly at the sand tray; audio-tapes of conversations at the dough table or musical patterns played on the piano; narrative observations following specific incidents or activities in which we have been involved; time or incident samples maintained throughout the day on specific children or specific actions; photographs and children's own recorded work – all can make an important contribution to the emerging three-dimensional picture of children's mathematical thinking. In this way staff can plan to play an active role in taking children's mathematical learning forward. The dynamic nature of education is such that in the process staff will themselves learn more, both about mathematics and about learning.

Planning for mathematical learning and thinking

Political pressures

In accepting a developmental approach to the curriculum for young children, the highest priority must be given to the needs and development of the individual child.

(Lally 1991: 86)

For those who view the development of young children and the provision of a curriculum designed to support that development appropriately as paramount, the current political climate creates conflicts which some find difficult to resolve. In practice there are many downward pressures on those who work with young children to work towards the objectives set and defined for older children. Indeed, it has been said that pressure emanating from universities is shaping the curriculum of the nursery. A story told by Pat Gura and Tina Bruce of an observation from the Froebel Blockplay Research Project serves as a reminder of the ineptness of this stance:

a recent three-year-old arrival to the nursery class had been watching with awe-struck admiration as an older child was completing a tall and magnificent block structure by standing on a stepladder. The newcomer was anxious to emulate this daring achievement, picked up a block, climbed to the top of the ladder and asked, 'Can I start here?'

Downward pressures have emanated from the National Curriculum (Cox and Sanders 1994) and from the desirable learning outcomes (SCAA 1996). In some early childhood settings, adults now feel that their planning must be all about specific objectives. To do this, to define specific learning objectives divorced from the learning needs of children, is to fly in the face of two centuries of growth in the understanding of young children's minds. As early childhood practitioners, we face a difficult task. We need to place, side by side, the learning needs of children and the things that society expects them to know. We should never lose sight of the fact that children must become not only literate and numerate but flexible, resourceful and confident mathematicians.

Subject knowledge

Aubrey (1994: 68) comments that in the area of mathematics, teachers are helped to plan in such a way as to enable them to react to children's learning needs if they are confident in the relevant subject knowledge. She says they will then have a mental plan or agenda of what they hope children will learn and a curriculum script so that they know how to turn their subject knowledge into effective classroom practice.

The problem with mathematics is that many of the adults who work with young children lack confidence in their own abilities in this area of the curriculum. Lally (1991: 86) writes:

> many teachers say that their own negative feelings about subjects such as science can limit their approach to children's learning in this area. They also say that exploring and discovering alongside young children has been the most effective science teaching they have received.

Subject knowledge can help those who work with young children to be more relaxed about helping them to achieve it. Gura (1994) has criticized a subject-based approach. While recognizing the value of subject expertise, her concerns are about the way in which the curriculum for young children becomes shaped by the subjects, rather than building on what we know of young children's learning. Aubrey (1994) says that subject specialists in the early years tend to teach their specialist area more dynamically, represent the subject in more varied ways, encourage and respond more fully to children's questions and comments. Her views are in part echoed by Menmuir and Adams (1997: 34):

> These intentions cannot be too specific or they may limit the inquiry but the better the underlying understanding of maths which the adult possesses, the easier it is to recognise the mathematical potential of a wide range of children's persistent concerns.

It is vital that early childhood specialism is equally valued alongside subject expertise, as Menmuir and Adams intimate. In a recent article, exploring the role of subject knowledge in Reggio Emilia, where each school employs an *atelierista* or art specialist, Pound and Gura (1997) write:

> it is clear that when expertise is co-ordinated, the effects, as in Reggio Emilia, are felt not only in terms of particular areas of knowledge and skill but in the *connections* which can be made between ideas and people.

Approaches to planning

At all stages of planning it is vital that teachers create activities that are engaging and interesting in their own right and that offer a real-life context for each aspect of maths.

(Lewis 1996: 179)

Planning for mathematics needs to happen at many levels. Over the course of a year or more, depending on how long most children attend the setting, there will be a range of areas that you will wish children to experience. These will include both the content curriculum – pattern and the search for relationships, measurement (including time), shape and space, counting (including work on money) – and the learning curriculum. Little of this planned mathematical activity will happen in isolation. The ongoing themes of children's education as a whole will be exploited and developed to ensure that each child's entitlement to the way of knowing and understanding the world which is mathematics is guaranteed.

Over the course of a month or a half-term, some specific plans will be laid to address these broad areas. For example, plans to visit a local farm will lead to planning for specific opportunities for mathematical development, among other things. Individual children will connect with these opportunities in different ways. To aid clearing up and to give a context for using numbers, 4-year-old James's teacher prepared small boxes which fitted inside the normal large storage trays. Attractively presented, each small box was labelled with a photograph and caption showing how many and what type of animal should be placed in it. James enjoyed playing with the small-world materials but was horrified when it was suggested to him that he might use these to make sure that all the farm animals were safely tidied away. 'I don't know numbers', he said. Wisely the teacher did not press his immediate involvement but began to observe. Over time the staff team realized that he had quite a lot of number knowledge but that he lacked confidence in using it because he was not as knowledgeable as his older sister. Future planning addressed his particular needs alongside the options for developing mathematics around the current theme or topic.

At this stage of education, structure is something which must exist in the *mind* of the adult – it must not be allowed to become an obstacle to learning. Having planned the content and learning curricula, the learning needs of the children must remain of paramount importance. Skilled teachers will ensure that the curriculum for each child matches their developmental needs by selecting material from the pre-planned components. When the planned learning opportunities are based on sensitive observation of children they will generally be developmentally appropriate. Sometimes unplanned chances to teach aspects of the planned content or learning curriculum will emerge. On other occasions, teachers will need to abandon planned activities, seeking other teaching requirements when children will be more receptive. There can be no justification for imposing on little children a series of undifferentiated worksheets. Nor should we believe that simply moving children in groups around a series of narrow mathematical tasks which are not designed to meet the specific learning needs of any of them will support their mathematical development. Learning must build on what they know and must therefore be individualized. 'Individualized' does not mean isolated and it certainly does not rule out the importance of joint discussions about mathematics – any more than the fact that children are at different stages of understanding stories means that they all have to have individual stories. Rather adults will need to be aware that different children will benefit differently from group sessions.

Supporting mathematical learning and thinking

Adults will have to wear a good many hats in undertaking their role of supporting mathematical learning and thinking. It is a broad issue and one which cannot be divorced from all the other support which they must give as children grow and develop as learners in all areas of experience and understanding. Many of the aspects discussed below are common to all other areas of learning.

Creating an ethos for mathematical learning

This demands the creation of an atmosphere within the classroom which values creative, flexible thought and which promotes approaches which will give lifelong support to thinking mathematically. It will, as a by-product, support other kinds of learning. Lewis (1996: 179) suggests that it is the role of the early childhood educator to develop a climate for learning. In such an ethos, children are enabled to take responsibilities and intellectual risks, to be independent and to make choices. Such a setting will be mutually supportive and will promote trust among its members. This will involve the professional in building on the children's own ideas. From them discussion, exploration, thought and imagination will all flow. Menmuir and Adams (1997) identify key elements in making enquiry happen. These include listening to and observing children and encouraging them to share their successes. Such encouragement will come through talking to parents and carers about what they have achieved. It will come through records, accessible to parents and children, which celebrate mathematical achievement in its broadest sense. It may come through displays in the classroom or early years setting giving a high profile to things that children have said about numbers or made using mathematical ideas. Books made by adults and children together about investigations or problem-solving activities will provide another strategy for sharing children's mathematical successes.

An important part of creating an ethos for mathematical learning is in ensuring that children have adults to whom they readily refer. Munn and Schaffer (1993) studied young children in day nurseries. They emphasize the value of a key worker system, with children assigned to one specific adult. They also suggest that teachers should stress early numeracy experiences, as they do with literacy. Teachers' ability to do so depended on their understanding of the role of talk and interaction in promoting children's mathematical learning.

Holding high but attainable expectations

Mathematical learning will be supported by having high expectations – like all developmental processes mathematical thinking develops, to a large extent, in response to the cultural context of the child. If we work to create a classroom where the implicit expectation is that children are destined to be competent and confident mathematicians in the broadest sense, then we are well on the way to helping them achieve that. Part of having high expectations lies in not giving too much praise. The repetitive use of phrases such as 'That's lovely, dear!' and 'That's super!' can be patronizing and may not enable children to build on their successes or avoid failure in the future. Praise of this sort does not provide children with any information that will allow them to develop the strengths of what they have achieved. It can also make children feel that we are too easily pleased and not provide any incentive to struggle with ideas. Constructive criticism is, however, important and is most effective when it focuses on positive aspects. Where adults comment on the things which children have done well – used a new strategy, managed to remember something previously discussed, successfully matched things up, identified a pattern – this allows children to reflect on what they have done and do it again. At some points, children will benefit from an addition to these positive comments which asks them to reflect further – perhaps adding 'Can you think of any other ways of doing that?' or 'Is that the only pattern you can see?'. The combination of specific praise and challenge can encourage children to ask more of themselves.

With young children, who are so vulnerable to the intentions of adults and so anxious to please, it is easy to promote 'prediction and other mathematical thinking processes by drawing attention to them as they arise' (Lewis 1996: 179). We must take care that we do not signal to children the overriding importance of things which may inhibit their long-term development as mathematicians. They are all too eager to please us and if we signal that doing pages of sums is what we most value, many will want to do that. Girls, in particular, may enjoy keeping busy, doing unchallenging but safe activities, which frequently result in praise and rows of ticks. High expectations are not all about getting things right. If children do not make mistakes, they will not be learning. Their errors show adults what their thinking is and thus enables them to support children's learning.

Promoting mental images

Lewis (1996) further suggests that conversations and planned activities should encourage children to develop mental images, rather than always relying on concrete apparatus. Activities based on Martin Hughes's (1986a) tins with small bricks placed inside are a good example of such activities. Over time, beginning with real bricks going into the tin, children developed the ability to imagine the bricks even when none were visible. Numberlines and number squares and the use of fingers or structured apparatus as memory aids can provide the basis for reflective thought – providing visual cues or, in Brown's (1996) term, *metaphors* for thinking.

Encouraging discussion

Clarke and Atkinson (1996) emphasize the importance of talk in promoting mathematical thinking. Adults, they suggest, should monitor their own contributions and use tangible materials to support verbal explanations, particularly for young children, those learning English as an additional language and those who may be experiencing language delay or disorders. They suggest encouraging children to talk about their current understanding and to explore things they do not understand.

The tension between providing visual cues and encouraging children to rely on thought without external aids should be explored. In fact the work of Martin Hughes (1986a) provides a good model. Habit and routine played a part in the process he established. Teachers might begin by putting, for example, three blocks into a bag, making their actions highly visible. They might add three more – with larger-than-life actions so that all children will be aware exactly what has happened. This game, for this is what it should be, may be played over a considerable period. Only when children are really familiar with it should the prop of the actual blocks be pulled away, so that those who are unsure can still gain enjoyment. If the group is small enough to ensure that no one has to wait too long for a turn, harder challenges may be offered to individual children. A balance needs to be struck between keeping the group, on the one hand, large and diverse enough so that children are exposed to a range of understandings and, on the other hand, compact enough for children to feel personally involved.

Intervening or interfering?

Clarke and Atkinson (1996) suggest that children should be encouraged to offer explanations to each other, accepting everyone's contribution, thus keeping adult intervention in such conversations to a minimum. Lewis (1996: 179) also urges against intervention when it is concerned with stepping in when children are heading for mistakes. Sometimes voicing their thinking can of itself help children to identify the inconsistencies in their own understanding.

Intervention is, however, vital in many contexts. Adults can provide explanations, sometimes supported by analogies to help make the explanations clearer. Aubrey (1994: 68) claims that adults' subject knowledge plays a crucial role in their ability to do this effectively. They will have a key role in helping children to make connections, which will include the links with existing knowledge as well as the links with other areas of experience. When talking about bygone events, discussing with children the ways in which time is quantified, adults can encourage children to wrestle with that very complex concept. Although young children have very hazy ideas of distance – how many of us have experienced, either as a child or as a parent, the woebegone cry of 'Are we there yet?' – discussion about how far it is to the post office or Spain or India gives the adult an insight into the child's understanding. It also gives children an opportunity to test out their views on a sympathetic audience and to compare and modify their view in the light of what other children think.

Questioning is a common intervention strategy. It works best in promoting mathematical thought if the questions are open. A closed question which really only has one right answer – 'How many sheep are there?' – may tell us whether children can count to a specific number, unless they are enjoying being able to tell a sheep from a lamb. However, if they resent the question as being too obvious, or for some other more hidden reason, it will tell us little. Wood (1991) reminds us that questioning is not a wholly productive method of teaching young children. He suggests that children as young as 4 are often aware when adults already know the answer to the questions they ask. He continues:

> The less a teacher interrogates children, the more likely they are to listen to, make contributions about and ask questions of what the other children say . . . The extent to which a child reveals his or her own ideas and seeks information is thus inversely proportional to the

frequency of teacher questions – and this finding embraces studies of pre-school children through to 16 year olds, deaf children and children acquiring English as a second language.

(Wood 1991: 115)

Open questions which children recognize as having a variety of answers and to which we genuinely do not have a specific answer will motivate thought and stimulate a spirit of enquiry. Lewis (1996: 179) suggests questioning *right* answers so that children develop the habit of justifying and explaining their views.

Intervening for equality of opportunity

Teachers and other professionals will need to evaluate their practice in the light of the need to ensure equality of opportunity. As Kelly (1994: 22) writes, citing Warnock:

> there is a difference between claiming that everyone has an equal right to education and that everyone has a right to equal education. In a democratic society 'entitlement' should mean more than entitlement to access; it should mean entitlement to full and appropriate provision.

The disabled, those with marked mathematical aptitude, girls and boys, those for whom English is an additional language and those of all social classes and levels of privilege have a right to an education that makes them not simply numerate but able to think mathematically. They also should be given access to the exciting and challenging aspects of mathematics which will remain for ever closed to most of today's adult population. Children who cannot move freely may enjoy the power of commanding a computer-controlled robot or vehicle. Those who are in the early stages of learning English will benefit from a chance to talk in their first language with their peers about the ideas and concepts they are being encouraged to develop in English.

Adults' evaluation will include a check to ensure that the needs of all the learners in the class are being met. Traditionally mathematics has been seen as an area in which boys excel and free choice is sometimes criticized as merely prolonging stereotypical behaviour. Parkin's (1991: 63) observations in her classroom led her to the following conclusions:

> The free choice of young infants does not differ significantly between girls and boys but there is a difference in the way boys and girls behave and in the way they use resources. Girls' behaviour prevents them participating equally with boys in many problem-solving and

other practical classroom activities but their behaviour is advantageous to other expressions of mathematical concepts. In certain mathematical activities girls perform as well as and sometimes better than boys.

In the blockplay project (Gura 1992) adults found that where they involved themselves in children's play and where children were given time and space to explore the materials exhaustively stereotypical behaviour disappeared.

If children are not making progress is it because the curriculum has not engaged them? Cousins (1990: 30–31) describes Sonnyboy's difficulties in accessing the curriculum of his reception class:

He was scathing about the absence of real money in the classroom shop; couldn't fathom out what was meant by playtime; questioned why school scissors were always blunt and didn't see why you couldn't eat snacks when you felt hungry. He put on extra clothes for PE because it was cold in the hall and decided assembly was the time to dream . . . School time caused him a lot of trouble . . .

Writers in Britain and abroad have documented social class differences in young children's mathematical achievement around the age of compulsory schooling (Hughes 1986a; Young-Loveridge 1987), with children from advantaged socio-economic circumstances demonstrating greater levels of knowledge. Results nationally throughout the years of schooling reflect this difference. However, the research of Tizard et al. (1988) suggested that even when children from disadvantaged groups entered school with higher measured levels of achievement they did ultimately less well than other more advantaged children. Walkerdine (1989) offers explanations which have to do with the constraints which poverty and low status impose on families. Others would suggest that teachers have lower expectations of children in disadvantaged circumstances. There are no easy answers to these complex findings, but if equality of access has any meaning at all, practitioners have a responsibility to ensure that every aspect of the child's previous experience is valued and developed.

Scaffolding

Bruner (1983: 60) picks up Vygotsky's notion of *scaffolding* and emphasizes the importance of adults playing a fully participatory role in children's learning. He writes:

If the teacher . . . were to have a motto, it would surely be *where before there was a spectator, let there now be a participant*. One . . . provides a scaffold to ensure that the child's ineptitudes can be rescued by appropriate intervention, and then removes the scaffold part by part as the reciprocal structure can stand on its own.

Wood (1991: 109) describes this as *leading by following*, meaning that scaffolds work best when they surround a structure that the child is interested in scaling. Scaffolding is a vital element in creating a developmentally appropriate curriculum. Wood (1991: 111) further reminds us that children as young as 9 months understand that adults (or older children) can be enlisted to offer the scaffold or support that they need to achieve something they want to do. At this tender age they are already capable of demonstrating that fierce combination of independence and interdependence that will mark out the effective learner.

Hutchin (1996: 104) offers helpful insights into some of the effective ways in which adults can scaffold children's experiences. She describes Faisal's mathematical development at the age of 3 years 3 months, and outlines what she sees as the implications for teaching:

Observation on Faisal:	*Implications for teaching*
F. lined up cars parallel to each other in rows, sorted out all the small cuboid blocks and lined them up similarly, talking in Bengali as he does this. Made a wall two rows with milk cartons at milk table, later made a similar pattern with blocks. Fitted cars on a flat board in rows covering all of surface, counted to 3 in English. When drawing, draws parallel horizontal lines on paper, usually doing several at one time.	Build on interest in parallel lines and lengths in lots of situations – e.g. rolling dough, collage, train set, large blocks outside. *Draw his models to show him the patterns* he makes. Continue interest in block play.

What is particularly interesting about the implications for teaching is the suggestion that the teacher should draw Faisal's model. Hutchin does not suggest that Faisal should be asked to do this, since Faisal has already represented his ideas. The teacher's drawings are to be used to focus his attention on a particular teaching point – not as a mechanism for keeping him at the model table for longer. It is the opportunity for interactive dialogue which is seen as important.

Demonstrating mathematical behaviour

Of great importance is the role that adults play as mathematicians themselves in supporting young children's mathematical learning. This will involve lifelong learning both about mathematics and about the process of learning itself. It will also involve modelling mathematical behaviour. Demonstrating the strategies used when counting up the dinner numbers or totalling the photograph money, writing number operations as you do them and so on will help children to see where and how we use mathematics.

Merttens (1996: 21–2) comments on the role that Piaget's work has played in undervaluing the role of adults in promoting mathematical thinking and in over-emphasizing the importance of commercially produced materials:

> Piaget's emphasis on children as lone individuals, all necessarily working at their own pace . . . hindered the role that interaction with peers played in the learning process . . . and obstructed the development of children's ability to make decisions about what they do, how and when – in short to think mathematically.

Merttens (1996: 10) also emphasizes that 'teaching is not telling'. She describes it as an *interactive process*, a dialogue. Unfortunately, from the point of view of those who care for and educate very young children, these useful statements are preceded by a section where the teacher's role in instructing, modelling, explaining, questioning and narrating is explored, in that order. It is a pity that she begins with instruction since for young children that is rarely a good starting point. Their questions and the adults' answers, explanations and illustrative stories are far more effective. Instruction, as discussed earlier, is most effective when it begins with the child's concerns. The younger the child, the more important it is that adults' instruction matches the child's immediate needs.

Observing, planning and supporting

A nursery unit had been focusing on boats and were placing a special emphasis on *Mr. Gumpy's Outing* (Burningham 1972) with props to support role play, materials for small-world play and magnetic cut-outs to use on a story board. Some children had been making boats, and during a group story session the nursery nurse discussed with them the boats that some of the children had made. Several of the children had difficulty in remembering the word for the sail. Suddenly 3-year-old Danny remembered it – 'It's a triangle sail!'. Each time the nursery nurse commented on a sail, he would add that it was a triangle. At the team meeting the nursery nurse talked to the rest of the team about the session. It was decided that some plastic boats, some of which had square sails, would be put in the water tray and that Danny would be invited to join in the making of a book about boats using pictures of boats with a range of sails in order to help him clarify the meaning of the two words.

Ten-month-old Siân was observed to enjoy play with things that rolled. Her key worker talked to Siân's parent about it, who said that she had a small clear plastic ball at home with bells inside. She liked to push it with her hand and crawl after it. Staff asked the parent if he would like to bring it in to the nursery. They found a similar one with coloured fish inside. Siân's enjoyment of the similarities and differences was evident.

Four-year-old Mei enjoyed using a computer program which required children to match a number of objects to a number symbol. If the number of objects displayed did not match, some more could be added by pressing the space bar, or taken away by pressing the delete key. Mei's strategy was to empty the box on the screen by pressing the delete key and then to put in as many as she needed. So, for example, if the number was 8 but six objects were displayed she would delete all six and then count to 8 as she added in objects. Staff had observed this over a period of several days but then noticed that in checking how many cartons of milk were left she was able to count on. She had been asked to check how many cartons were left on the trolley, which she did telling staff that there were six. She then added, however, that there were two more on the table so there were eight altogether. In order to help her to connect her understanding to the computer program, the teacher prepared an activity for a small group following a story session. Specific numbers of objects were hidden in a bag and a small number added. Among the objects used were included some of the things that were used on the computer program in order to help Mei to transfer her understanding.

Summary

Those who recognize the need to offer young children a developmentally appropriate curriculum seek to build on the 'natural' ways of learning which operate between young children and their parents or carers (Papousek and Papousek 1987). Where parents are under stress, this unconsciously driven pattern of interaction, where parents build on what they see children do and offer support for them to do things which are just a little beyond their capability, may break down.

Professional carers and educators work to conflicting sets of demands and may be less focused in their intentions than parents. They have also to care for larger numbers of children with less intimate knowledge than parents have. Planning therefore becomes of vital importance since it allows parents to negotiate where potential conflicts arise and the practitioners themselves to ensure that entitlements are offered to all.

6

Parents and professionals working together

Children need 'warm demanders' if they are to thrive
(Ball 1994: 43)

'Partnerships' has become an easy word: on all sides we are exhorted to develop them – business partnerships, development partnerships and, not least, home–school partnerships. Fortunately overuse of the word does not make them less valuable, but neither does it make them any easier to achieve. Whether easy or difficult to achieve, partnership between the parents of young children and those who work with them in early years settings is not negotiable – it is absolutely essential. The knowledge which parents have of their own children's experiences, preferences and growing understanding is vital to staff's awareness. The records which staff keep of children's growing understanding provides an important bridge, giving parents insight into the work of the early years setting. In relation to mathematics it becomes even more important, since so often the experiences of parents lead them to look for formal recording or sums as evidence of mathematics. Observations and assessments then support the close contact between the two groups responsible for the child's care and education which is essential if the child is to make the necessary connections between experiences at home and those elsewhere. Hughes (1986b: 36) writes:

[C]hildren grow up within a closely linked network of people, based on their family, which makes up their community. Much of children's early learning takes place within this network. When they start school, children find themselves in a very different world, from which there are few links either to their own community or to the kind of knowledge they have acquired within that community. One of the tasks of school must be to help children create these links. This will not be an easy task, and schools will need all the help they can get – particularly from parents.

What both family and workers have in common is that they want the best for the child. Among workers, teachers and others concerned with children's care and education within an institution, this concern is professional and largely objective. Among parents and others close to children within the close-knit circle of family and friends this desire is subjective and passionate. This is its strength (Bronfenbrenner 1979).

The educational benefits of contact between home and other carers and educators have been well expressed in a number of studies. Widlake and Macleod (1984: 49) quote the words of an unnamed community educator in the United States:

> There is a whole book of studies . . . that makes very interesting reading. Fifty-five pages of short versions of studies that say when parents take any interest in schooling, the kids' ranks go up; even if they only spend ten minutes a day talking about school; even if they only wish the kids a good day and remind them to 'work hard today'.

One of the less well-known factors in the very well-publicized long-term effects of the High/Scope Project was the close involvement of parents. Staff were given significant allocations of time to make home visits, to develop contact and to discuss children's progress with their parents.

Barriers to partnership

There are many things that make partnership difficult. One is the lack of training among professionals for working *with* parents. There is a danger that in a profession with low status (and sometimes low morale), some will seek to hold on to the small amount of power that they have and will not wish to share it with parents. Gillian Pugh (1985) has commented on the fact that professionals often unwittingly damage parents' self-confidence. If this is true in general, it is certainly true about mathematics. Parents as a representative part of the population will not be exempt from the insecurity that many people feel about their ability to make use of mathematics in their everyday lives. On top of that insecurity, Burton (1994: 124) reminds us that 'parents have to make two major shifts in their thinking'.

First, *what* children learn, what is called mathematics, is likely to look very different for all but the youngest parents from what they themselves experienced at school. Second, *how* children are taught, and the organization of the classroom including mathematical resources, is likely to differ from some parents' very unhappy memories of mathematics teaching. Stein (1989) points out that, paradoxically, even when parents' experience of mathematics at school has been unhappy or unsuccessful, they are wary of urging change in either the content or the teaching approach and would prefer things to remain as they were in a system that failed them.

A further barrier to partnership in relation to the development of children's mathematical thinking is alluded to by Browne (1991: 18). She focuses on the difficulties for early childhood practitioners in teaching science, but in doing so highlights the common issues raised in relation to mathematics. Practitioners are said to be afraid of not being able to answer children's questions or of not being able to help children find their own answers. They are, moreover, frightened of the mathematics that might be involved in young children's science questions. The combination of parental distrust of change in the teaching of mathematics and practitioners' lack of confidence will magnify the difficulties associated with partnership and make it unlikely that professionals will feel able either to negotiate change or to convince parents of a need to do so.

Parents' views of course should not be seen as a homogeneous whole. Their views will form a continuum from those who fear mathematics and who do not mind if their children are not good at it to those who have very high expectations. Clemson and Clemson (1994: 23) suggest that young children have an implicit sense of their parents' views of mathematics. Some will know that their parents do not like mathematics. Some will have gained the impression that mathematics is hard while others will be equally sure that it is easy, especially boys. For some, to be good at counting and sums will be seen as important; while for others, they will be an irrelevance. Some will be very clear that this is an area in which their parents wish them to succeed, even though it is hard. The views of parents interviewed by Atkinson (1992: 165) reflect a similar range:

> I panic about maths. As I am talking to you now my heart is pounding . . . if maths is mentioned, I go all hot and cold. I cannot help my own children, because I panic as soon as they tell me the problem. I want them to understand not just be told to learn it by rote . . . Most of all I don't want them to panic like I did.

> I wasn't any good at maths so I don't suppose my child will be either.

> They do things like cooking at school, and lots of practical maths, but now she is seven, I want her to get on with some real maths.

> I don't want my child to suffer what I went through. I want her to enjoy it and understand it.

> I don't approve of all this messing about with shapes and cubes.

Supporting partnership

Because we know that children from families who give mathematics a high profile in their day-to-day lives (Young-Loveridge 1989) develop a greater enthusiasm for mathematics, early childhood practitioners should be doing all they can to encourage parents to play games, talk about time, and draw children's attention to calendars, money and telephone numbers when they are using them. Early childhood educators have, however, an additional responsibility, namely to replicate these conditions which lead to children becoming *young experts* (Young-Loveridge 1989). Where young children are in full-day care it is especially important that they are given frequent and varied opportunities to use the real-life mathematics prevalent in the real-life situation of the home: in cooking, handling money, checking bus numbers for journeys, remembering phone numbers and making sure that there are sufficient quantities of everything.

What parents do best (Stein 1989) is give their children real-life contexts for mathematics. 'It is the school's role to introduce children to a way of thinking and knowing the world which is independent of their own experiences' (Tizard and Hughes 1984: 263). These things can only be achieved if schools value and build on the real experiences that children have. Independence from their own experiences can only come about when we have encouraged children to see the connections between their contextualized learning and the more abstract understandings we wish them to move towards. The attitude of their parents is part of that link.

A further example of where we may fail to build on children's prior learning may lie in the emphasis given to sorting, matching and ordering, claims Womack (1993). He writes that 'it is more than likely that the average home environment provides a sufficient variety of these activities'. Others (Gifford 1995; Macnamara 1996; Merttens 1996) support him in thinking that the early emphasis given to these activities, particularly in reception classes, represents a failure to recognize children's prior experiences.

The insecurities that exist on both parts can lead to unrealistic demands – some low expectations from professionals, as Womack's work seems to indicate, and some unhelpful expectations on the part of parents. One parent, quoted in Atkinson (1992: 165) as saying 'You're failing my child. She is four, in the nursery, and she doesn't know her tables yet', provides an example.

Somehow the oft-quoted words of the Cockcroft Report (DES 1982; cited in Lewis 1996: 173) have not gained much credence:

> Albeit with the best of intentions, parents can exert undesirable pressure on teachers to introduce written recording in mathematics . . .

A premature start on formal, written arithmetic is likely to delay progress rather than hasten it.

There can be no doubt that the political emphasis on high achievement has increased parental anxiety. In a study by David (1992) the views of Belgian and British parents on pre-school education were compared. The former placed an emphasis on children developing naturally, while British parents placed importance on the early development of reading and writing. Cox and Sanders (1994: 176) suggest that this shows a need for

> nursery educators to demonstrate to parents that the informal learning experiences that characterize early childhood education yield real and observable benefits for the children, even though they precede the more formal achievements.

The Rumbold Report (DES 1990: para. 100) underlines this point:

> What is needed is for educators to be able and willing to explain to parents how the experiences offered to children contribute to their learning, and to describe how their children are progressing . . . They must ensure that they have the necessary skills to work effectively with parents . . . There is much to be done if early childhood education is to make its contribution to improving the quality of mathematical education both in what actually happens in early childhood settings but also in convincing parents of the reasons for doing what we do in early childhood settings. This will not be easy since many practitioners find it very difficult to articulate the rationale for the way in which they work.

Developing communication with parents

For many parents, working alongside children in an early years setting can help them to understand what teaching staff are trying to achieve. They may supervise specific activities, help to display work, work with children on the computer or read to them. This can be particularly useful where the parent has worries about too much play and not enough work, although, as the parent quoted by Atkinson (1992: 165) shows, this strategy is by no means foolproof. The parent says 'I go in to help some days and they ask me to play maths games. I quite enjoy doing that and the children love it, but it is not real maths, is it?' Parents need to have explained the purpose of what they are being asked to do. One wonders whether this parent had been asked, for example, to observe the strategies that children were using or to encourage children to guess the number of spots on the dice before counting them in order to promote speed, estimation and confidence.

With older children, Burton (1994) recommends encouraging them to record their work (in, for example, scoring games or describing how sweets have been fairly distributed) in order to show their parents what they have been doing. She also suggests that teachers make sure that children are aware of the mathematics they have been doing so that they are able to tell their parents about it. In the case of younger children, adults working with them will need to undertake this kind of link themselves. This is partly because children may not have the language to do it successfully, but it is also because such conversations give parents an opportunity to raise questions and to share views with staff.

From these conversations, staff may decide that it would be helpful to focus on certain aspects of the mathematics curriculum. In order to do this they may develop parent workshops or open evenings where parents may be given the chance to use equipment and generally try out some of the experiences their children are having. In some nurseries, leaflets raising pertinent issues are published and distributed to parents.

Regular information about the mathematics curriculum may be conveyed to parents. Many early years settings have a curriculum noticeboard or regular newsletter to keep parents up to date with plans for all areas of the curriculum including mathematics. Booklets outlining the approach to maths taken by staff can also be helpful. For example, the Robert Owen Nursery School produced a booklet for parents to help them support their own children's mathematical development. This included examples of what the school did to promote mathematical thinking, and also offered ideas for ways in which parents could help at home. Similarly, the HBJ Mathematics scheme (Kerslake *et al.* 1990) includes draft format letters to parents explaining what aspect of mathematics is to be taught during the coming half term. The letter for each topic includes four headings: 'What we will be doing'; 'Why we will be doing it'; 'How you can help'; and 'Try this at home!'.

Instead of simply informing parents about the mathematics curriculum, early childhood educators could try asking for their suggestions. Again the ensuing conversations may do much to promote mutual understanding, as can the practice of inviting parents to contribute to their child's own record. Parents' insights into children's mathematical understanding may take a different stance than those contributed by professionals and the merging of ideas can be helpful. This two-way exchange of ideas can be especially helpful where the culture of the home and that of the school differ. It is clear from research (Stein 1989) that understandings of mathematics are likely to be different among families and workers, but this gulf may be particularly significant where parents have been educated outside Britain. Staff will need to show particular sensitivity and be willing to spend time explaining why mathematics is being approached in the way that it is. For their part, parents will need to give staff insight into what is being done at home.

Home reading schemes, with children regularly borrowing books, are well established in many early years settings. An increasingly important way of developing shared understandings with parents about children's mathematical thinking and knowledge is to encourage children to take activities such as investigations, games and puzzles home to share with their family. Burton (1994: 131) quotes from a letter to parents designed to encourage their involvement in what is sometimes called an IMPACT scheme:

> The home is where a child's maths education begins. It also provides a wealth of opportunities for maths activities and games. Here, you and your child can be together in a relaxed setting which is relevant to the child. It also offers you a chance to share maths with your child without too much extra effort!

The involvement of parents can be further enhanced if parents themselves are active in making games and resources for a home lending scheme. Simple board games with a variety of dice – some with spots, some with numbers, some with pictures and some even with words – are simple to play at home and can be undertaken by older brothers and sisters as well as parents and grandparents. The kits and patterns for resources produced by Zöe Evans (1986) are examples of the sorts of materials which parents can enjoy producing for use at home and at school. Variations on the large sets of snakes and ladybirds with a variety of attributes to promote mathematical comparison, which Evans and the parents at her school produced, could be used at home. In addition, the literacy packs (a book together with props, which might be a toy related to the story, a relevant game or a set of small characters which represent the characters in the book) produced by some nurseries and schools to support reading at home can have applications for developing mathematical understanding. The set of animals which accompanies *Rosie's Walk* (Hutchin 1968) in such a pack, for example, offers lots of opportunities for mathematical discussion and language. Similarly, some early years settings produce props for number rhymes including such favourites as 'Five fat sausages sizzling in a pan' (sausages made from tights fastened with Velcro to a cardboard frying pan) and 'Five little speckled frogs'. These props are generally confined to the early years classroom but some parents might be happy to make replicas which could be used at home – thus sharing familiar songs and rhymes as well as mathematics. Hand-manufactured books with a mathematical theme, perhaps illustrating a recent educational visit focusing on shape, depicting activities where patterns are discernible or encouraging counting of resources in the setting, might also be popular materials for use at home. By enabling the child to talk about nursery at home they have the additional virtue of linking home and school in quite explicit ways.

Merttens and Vass (1990) are of the view that parents should be encouraged to make written responses when they have used mathematics materials at home. Early childhood educators will want to consider the extent to which they feel this is worthwhile. There is an opportunity for conversation with a child's parent or carer on most days, and these chats, sometimes very informal, can be invaluable. Demands for written responses may disadvantage parents who cannot read or write English or who do not find writing easy. However, a written record as an addition to regular face-to-face discussion has some merits. First, it invites the involvement of any parents who are not able to meet staff regularly. Second, it establishes a habit of written response which can be supportive as the child moves through primary schooling, where staff may see less of parents and may need mechanisms to keep in touch with parents. Some early years settings have resolved the issue by producing sheets which have columns with easily understood symbols which can be ticked or coloured, and may even be completed by the child with the support of the parent. A space may be added for those parents who wish to add a written comment.

If the staff of a particular setting feel that written responses would be useful they will need to design a format with which parents will feel comfortable. In nurseries which are separate from primary schools, it may be useful to make contact in order to make some link between approaches adopted in the early years setting and those which will be adopted in the primary school. If more elaborate responses are sought, schools with bilingual populations may need to translate forms into relevant languages. They may also need to consider how monolingual staff can gain insight into parents' views.

Atkinson (1992: 23) describes 'helping children to make the links between home and school maths' as 'a vital and important task for teachers and parents in the maths education of children'. The younger the child the more this responsibility can realistically *only* be carried by the adults who have responsibility for their care and education. As children grow older, they may share in the task of linking home and school, but neither parents nor professionals should allow this to become a burden to the child which it will do if disagreement or conflict cloud the relationship. The Rumbold Report (DES 1990: para. 100) summarizes the role which professionals must take on:

They need to be able to share responsibility with parents. This places considerable demands upon the educators: they need to be ready to spend time on it, and to exercise sensitivity; they also need to have enough confidence to invite parents to share in their children's education.

Furthermore, within the partnership, professionals must take responsibility for ensuring that parents understand why this sharing is so vital to each child's future mathematical development and what role each of the partners can most helpfully play. Only by being fully aware of the child's total experience can parents and educators effectively challenge children's mathematical thinking.

Summary

The difficulties of maintaining a partnership between parents and professionals are heightened in relation to mathematics since parents often have fixed ideas about what counts as maths and professionals are often insecure and defensive about their own understanding of the subject. As professionals, early years carers and educators must, for the sake of the child's development, take a lead in involving parents. This will include a wide range of strategies – explaining, sharing planning and records, discussing, encouraging parents to play mathematical games and sing rhymes – in fact anything which will bring home and institutional settings closer and bridge the differences for the child.

Conclusion

> We need to help young children not to 'do' maths, but to use those mathematical tools created by the people of many cultures and centuries in order to recreate mathematics in their world and in this way to become young mathematicians.
>
> (Metz 1987: 201)

No one could deny that something is going wrong somewhere with mathematics education in Britain. Yet, as we have seen, young children are immensely competent. Something prevents many of them from achieving in later years the promise they showed as young children. The drive and determination which they show as young learners is rarely translated into enthusiasm for learning mathematics in primary and secondary schools. Hughes (1986a: 184) refers to this phenomenon as a challenge:

> We have on our side . . . a strength which is often underestimated: the immense capacity of young children to grasp difficult ideas if they are presented in ways which interest them and make sense to them. It is not always easy to design situations which meet these criteria but . . . the attempt to do so is usually worthwhile. If we can redesign our educational environments . . . so that, instead of nullifying and ignoring young children's strengths, we are able to bring them into play and build on them, then I am confident that we will be able to meet the challenge currently facing us.

Politicians, employers and educationalists whose main expertise lies in subjects of the curriculum or in working with older students may be sceptical about young children's strengths. However, parents and primary carers who are the experts on their own child's learning and early childhood specialists who have insight into young children's learning in general do not doubt it. We must therefore work together, in partnership, to convince everyone that we have answers to some of the dilemmas facing us.

The first task before early childhood practitioners is to convince ourselves that we have something to say which needs to be heard. The insights of the pioneers of early childhood education in Britain were based on observation. Their central tenets in relation to social interaction, the role of dialogue and the fundamental importance of physical thought in action are increasingly supported by research findings. These insights are crucial to our understanding of development, including the development of mathematical thinking. A developmentally appropriate curriculum, with its emphases on respect for children's individuality, on the need to engage with each child's individual starting point for learning and the vital involvement of parents in ensuring coherent experiences (Hurst and Joseph, 1998), builds on these insights.

Also crucial is the early childhood practice of interactive teaching – building on what children know and can do in order to help them learn more. Currently, external bodies are placing an emphasis on the curriculum map – the desirable learning outcomes, the National Numeracy Project and the National Curriculum all tell us where children must get to. This information is only useful if we are clear about where children are starting from and what interests and understandings are driving them. A railway map is of no value if you're travelling on a bicycle. It is important to know the destination but those who have defined it must remember two things. First, there are many routes – children's mathematical learning is not a ladder but more closely resembles a jigsaw. Second, children have to undertake the journey for themselves. Learning, including mathematical learning, is an active process and although adults may direct, instruct, cajole, demand, model, tell and ask, in the end the child is the one who determines what is learnt. This is in no way to suggest that adults do not have a crucial role to play in that learning process. But the support or scaffolding which they offer will be most effective when placed along the child's chosen route. Practitioners must observe, plan and implement a supportive approach which they think will help the child and then evaluate the extent to which it is helping learning.

At the same time, early childhood practitioners will also have to become more confident about their own mathematical abilities, since it is often insecurity which leads staff to fall back on the ways in which they were (often largely unsuccessfully) taught mathematics. This may be, as Lally (1991) has suggested, by learning alongside the children. It is increasingly evident that we all get better at doing things by doing them. It may also be, however, that we must learn to work in partnership with experts in mathematics. They may be surprised to find that they can learn from those who work with young children. In a recent article, Professor Shayer of King's College is quoted as saying:

We are moving towards a different way of teaching, not just of maths and science but of everything – one that is not just concerned with kids' conceptual knowledge but with the quality of their underlying thinking.

(Barnard 1997: 4)

Independence and discussion are seen as fundamental to the approach which he is advocating to science education. There is also an emphasis on helping children to think about how they learn. The legacy of the early childhood pioneers and the insights of early childhood practitioners will yet be vindicated!

Instruction has a role to play in learning but it cannot successfully operate outside the young child's concerns. The most skilful teachers of young children seize their opportunities, creating and exploiting the *teachable moments*. In this they have learnt from the intuitive teaching which occurs between parents and children in the home.

Vicky Hurst (1987: 109) has described parents' involvement in the education of their school-age children as 'the greatest single opportunity for educational advance'. Their involvement before and at the start of statutory schooling has even more potential. In relation to mathematics, the opportunities are immense. Working in partnership with parents, professionals can learn more about the children they teach and more about how they have learnt all that they know when they enter an early years setting. Parents can learn from professionals more about what counts as mathematics and why.

Learning to think mathematically is within the grasp of all. Those who have the privilege of working with young children and their families are part of the solution to the problem. We must, as did the pioneers of early childhood education, trust our insights and intuitions. However, we must also make our voices heard – thinking mathematically involves much more than mathematics. It depends upon a playful, reflective and respected start to learning.

References

Ainley, J. (1981) Playing games and real mathematics, in D. Pimm (ed.) *Mathematics Teachers and Children*. London: Hodder and Stoughton/The Open University.

Alexander, R. (1997) Basics, cores, margins and choices: towards a new primary curriculum, in *Developing the Primary School Curriculum: the Next Steps*. A collection of papers from an invitational conference held by the School Curriculum and Assessment Authority, 9–10 June 1997. London: SCAA.

Anghileri, J. (ed.) (1995) *Children's Mathematical Thinking in the Primary Years*. London: Cassell.

Athey, C. (1990) *Extending Thought in Young Children*. London: Paul Chapman.

Atkinson, S. (ed.) (1992) *Mathematics with Reason: The Emergent Approach to Primary Maths*. London: Hodder and Stoughton.

Atkinson, S. and Clarke, S. (1992a) The use of standard notation, in S. Atkinson (ed.) *Mathematics with Reason*. London: Hodder and Stoughton.

Atkinson, S. and Clarke, S. (1992b) Children's own mathematical representations, in S. Atkinson (ed.) *Mathematics with Reason*. London: Hodder and Stoughton.

Aubrey, C. (ed.) (1994) *The Role of Subject Knowledge in the Early Years of Schooling*. London: Falmer Press.

Baker, L. (1995) Re-solving problem solving, in J. Angilheri (ed.) *Children's Mathematical Thinking in the Primary Years*. London: Cassell.

Ball, C. (ed.) (1994) *Start Right – The Importance of Early Learning*. London: Royal Society of Arts.

Barnard, N. (1997) A learning revolution spreads, *Times Educational Supplement*, 17 October.

Bissex, G. (1980) *Gnys at Wrk*. London: Harvard University Press.

Blenkin, G. (1994) Early learning and a developmentally appropriate curriculum:

some lessons from research, in G. Blenkin and A. V. Kelly (eds) *The National Curriculum and Early Learning*. London: Paul Chapman.

Bloom, B. (1985) *Developing Talent in Young People*. New York: Ballantine.

Bloom, L. (1970) *Language Development: Form and Function in Emerging Grammars*. Cambridge, Mass.: MIT Press.

Bower, T. (1977) *The Perceptual World of the Child*. London: Fontana.

Bredekamp, S. (ed.) (1987) *Developmentally Appropriate Practice in Early Childhood Programs Serving Children from Birth through Age 8*. Washington, DC: National Association for the Education of Young Children.

Briggs, R. (1970) *Jim and the Beanstalk*. London: Hamish Hamilton.

Bronfenbrenner, U. (1979) *The Ecology of Human Development*. London: Harvard University Press.

Brown, T. (1996) Play and number, in R. Merttens (ed.) *Teaching Numeracy*. Leamington Spa: Scholastic.

Browne, N. (ed.) (1991) *Science and Technology in the Early Years*. Buckingham: Open University Press.

Bruce, T. (1987) *Early Childhood Education*. London: Hodder and Stoughton.

Bruce, T. (1991) *Time to Play in Early Childhood Education*. London: Hodder and Stoughton.

Bruce, T. (1994) Play, the universe and everything!, in J. Moyles (ed.) *The Excellence of Play*. Buckingham: Open University Press.

Bruner, J. (1983) *Child's Talk*. New York: Norton.

Bruner, J. (1986) *Actual Minds, Possible Worlds*. London: Harvard University Press.

Buck, L. (1996) *The Pound Park Experience*. London: Greenwich Education Service.

Burningham, J. (1972) *Mr. Gumpy's Outing*. London: Jonathan Cape.

Burton, L. (1994) *Children Learning Mathematics: Patterns and Relationships*. Hemel Hempstead: Simon and Schuster Education.

Butler, D. (1979) *Cushla and Her Books*. Sevenoaks: Hodder and Stoughton.

Carle, E. (1969) *The Very Hungry Caterpillar*. New York: Philomel.

Carr, M. (1992) *Maths for Meaning: Tracing a Path for Early Mathematics Development*. Hamilton, New Zealand: University of Waikato Centre for Science and Mathematics Research.

Carraher, T. N., Carraher, D. W. and Schliemann, A. D. (1991) Mathematics in the streets and in schools, in P. Light, S. Sheldon and M. Woodhead (eds) *Learning to Think*. London: Routledge.

Chiu, C., Hong, Y. and Dweck, C. (1994) Towards an integrative model of personality and intelligence: a general framework and some preliminary steps, in R. J. Sternberg and P. Ruzgis (eds) *Personality and Intelligence*. Cambridge: Cambridge University Press.

City of Westminster (not dated) *Great Expectations*. London: City of Westminster Education Department.

Clarke, S. and Atkinson, S. (1996) *Tracking Significant Achievement in Primary Mathematics*. London: Hodder and Stoughton.

Claxton, G. (1997) *Hare Brain and Tortoise Mind*. London: Fourth Estate.

Clay, M. (1975) *What Did I Write?* London: Heinemann.

Clemson, D. and Clemson, W. (1994) *Mathematics in the Early Years*. London: Routledge.

Cousins (1990) Are your little Humpty Dumpties floating or sinking? *Early Years*, 10(2): 23–38.

Cox, T. and Sanders, S. (1994) *The Impact of the National Curriculum on the Teaching of Five Year Olds*. London: Falmer Press.

David, T. (1992) What do parents want their children to learn in pre-school in Belgium and the UK? Paper presented at the XXth World Congress of OMEP, North Arizona University, Flagstaff, Ariz.

Davies, M. (1995) *Helping Children to Learn through a Movement Perspective*. London: Hodder and Stoughton.

Department for Education (1995) *The National Curriculum*. London: HMSO.

Department of Education and Science (1982) *Mathematics Counts* (Cockcroft Report). London: HMSO.

Department of Education and Science (1990) *Starting with Quality* (Rumbold Report). London: HMSO.

Devi, S. (1990) *Figuring*. London: Penguin.

Doman, G. and Doman, J. (1994) *How To Teach Your Baby Math*. New York: Avery Publishing Group.

Donaldson, M. (1976) *Children's Minds*. London: Fontana.

Duffy, B. (1998) *Supporting Creativity and Imagination in the Early Years*. Buckingham: Open University Press.

Dunn, J. (1988) *The Beginnings of Social Understanding*. Oxford: Blackwell.

Early Childhood Education Forum (1998) *Quality in Diversity in Early Learning*. London: National Children's Bureau.

Edgington, M., Fisher, J., Morgan, M., Pound, L. and Scott, W. (1998) *Interpreting the National Curriculum*. Buckingham: Open University Press.

Edwards, C. and Forman, G. (1993) Conclusion: Where do we go from here?, in C. Edwards, L. Gandini and G. Forman (eds) *The Hundred Languages of Children*. Norwood, NJ: Ablex.

Egan, K. (1988) *Primary Understanding*. London: Routledge.

Evans, Z. (1986) *Spot On: A Zöe Evans Maths Toy*. Exeter: Hendre Crafts.

Ferreiro, E. and Teberosky, A. (1979) *Literacy before Schooling*. London: Heinemann.

Fisher, J. (1996) *Starting from the Child?* Buckingham: Open University Press.

Gardner, H. (1993) *The Unschooled Mind*. London: Fontana.

Gelman, R. and Gallister, C. R. (1978) *The Child's Understanding of Number*. Cambridge, Mass., Harvard University Press.

Gifford, S. (1995) Number in early childhood. *Early Childhood Development and Care*, 109: 95–119.

Ginsburg, H. (1977) *Children's Arithmetic*. New York: Van Nostrand.

Goldschmied, E. (1990) *Heuristic Play with Objects, and Infants Learning*. London: National Children's Bureau.

Greenfield, S. (1996) *The Human Mind Explained*. London: Cassell.

Griffiths, R. (1994) Mathematics and play, in J. Moyles (ed.) *The Excellence of Play*. Buckingham: Open University Press.

Guha, M. (1987) Play in school, in G. Blenkin and A. V. Kelly (eds) *Early Childhood Education: A Developmental Curriculum*. London: Paul Chapman Publishing.

Gura, P. (ed.) (1992) *Exploring Learning: Young Children and Blockplay*. London: Paul Chapman.

Gura, P. (1994) Scientific and technological development in the early years, in G. Blenkin and A. V. Kelly (eds) *The National Curriculum and Early Learning*. London: Paul Chapman.

Hall, N., Gillen, J. and Greenhall, R. (1996) 'Don't cry, I ring the cop shop': young children's pretend telephone behaviours, in N. Hall and J. Martello (eds) *Listening to Children Think: Exploring Talk in the Early Years*. London: Hodder and Stoughton.

Hargreaves, D. and Colley, A. (1986) *The Psychology of Sex Roles*. London: Harper and Row.

Harrison, C. and Pound, L. (1996) Talking music: empowering children as musical communicators. *British Journal of Music Education*, 13: 233–42.

Harste, J., Woodward, V. and Burke, C. (1984) *Language Stories and Literacy Lessons*. Portsmouth, NH: Heinemann.

Haylock, D. and Cockburn, A. (1989) *Understanding Early Years Mathematics*. London: Paul Chapman.

Hughes, M. (1986a) *Children and Number*. Oxford: Basil Blackwell.

Hughes, M. (1986b) Young children learning in the community, in *Involving Parents in the Primary Curriculum*, Perspectives 24, pp. 28–37. Exeter: University of Exeter.

Hurst, V. (1987) Parents and professionals: partnerships in early childhood education, in G. Blenkin and A. V. Kelly (eds) *Early Childhood Education: A Developmental Curriculum*. London: Paul Chapman.

Hurst, V. and Joseph, J. (1998) *Supporting Early Learning: The Way Forward*. Buckingham: Open University Press.

Hutchin, V. (1996) *Tracking Significant Achievement in the Early Years*. London: Hodder and Stoughton.

Hutchins, P. (1968) *Rosie's Walk*. London: Bodley Head.

Joseph, J. (1993) Four-year-olds in school: cause for concern, in P. Gammage and J. Meighan (eds) *Early Childhood Education: Taking Stock*. Ticknall, Derbyshire: Education Now Co-operative.

Karmiloff-Smith, A. (1994) *Baby It's You*. London: Ebury Press.

Kelly, A. V. (1994) Beyond the rhetoric and the discourse, in G. Blenkin and A. V. Kelly (eds) *The National Curriculum and Early Learning*. London: Paul Chapman.

Kerslake, D., Burton, L., Harvey, R., Street, L. and Walsh, A. (1990) *HBJ Mathematics: Teacher's Resource Book*. London: Harcourt Brace Jovanovich.

Lally, M. (1991) *The Nursery Teacher in Action*. London: Paul Chapman.

Leeds Under Eights Service (1996) *Let's Get It Right: Dimensions of Quality Education and Care*. Leeds: Leeds City Council.

Lewis, A. (1996) *Discovering Mathematics with 4- to 7-Year-Olds*. London: Hodder and Stoughton.

Macnamara, A. (1996) From home to school – do children preserve their counting skills?, in P. Broadhead (ed.) *Researching the Early Years Continuum*. Clevedon: Multilingual Matters.

Malaguzzi, L. (1993) History, ideas and basic philosophy, in C. Edwards, L. Gandini and G. Forman (eds) *The Hundred Languages of Children*. Norwood, NJ: Ablex.

Malaguzzi, L. (1997) *Shoe and Meter*. Municipality of Reggio Emilia: Reggio Children.

McMillan, M. (1930) *The Nursery School*. London: Dent.

Meek, M. (1982) *Learning to Read*. London: Bodley Head.

Menmuir, J. and Adams, K. (1997) Young children's inquiry learning in mathematics. *Early Years*, 17(2): 34–9.

Merttens, R. (1996) *Teaching Numeracy: Maths in the Primary Classroom*. Leamington Spa: Scholastic.

Merttens, R. (1997) Chants would be a fine thing. *Times Educational Supplement*, 24 January.

Merttens, R. and Vass, J. (1990) *Sharing Maths Cultures*. Basingstoke: Falmer Press.

Metz, M. (1987) The development of mathematical understanding, in G. Blenkin and A. V. Kelly (eds) *Early Childhood Education: A Developmental Curriculum*. London: Paul Chapman.

Mithen, S. (1996) *The Prehistory of the Mind*. London: Thames and Hudson.

Montague-Smith, A. (1997) *Mathematics in Nursery Education*. London: David Fulton.

Montessori, M. (1912) *The Montessori Method*. London: Heinemann.

Moyles, J. (1994) *The Excellence of Play*. Buckingham: Open University Press.

Munn, P. (1994) Counter intelligence at work. *Times Educational Supplement*, 5 April.

Munn, P. and Schaffer, H. R. (1993) Literacy and numeracy events in social interactive contexts. *International Journal of Early Years Education*, 1(3): 61–80.

National Numeracy Project (1997a) *Draft Framework: Examples of What 5 Year Olds Should Be Able to Do*. London: NNP.

National Numeracy Project (1997b) *Hungarian Primary Mathematics Classes*. NNP Project Video.

Nunes, T. (1996) Learning mathematics in primary school: from informal to formal. Susan Isaacs lecture, presented to the University of London Institute of Education, 16 November.

Nutbrown, C. (1994) *Threads of Thinking*. London: Paul Chapman.

Odam, G. (1995) *The Sounding Symbol*. Cheltenham: Stanley Thornes.

Ofsted (1996) *Primary Subject Guidance*. London: Ofsted.

Ofsted (1997) *The Teaching of Number in Three Inner-urban LEAs*. London: Ofsted.

Owen, A. and Rousham, L. (1997) Maths – is that a kind of game for grown-ups? Understanding numbers in the early years, in D. Whitebread (ed.) *Teaching and Learning in the Early Years*. London: Routledge.

Paley, V. G. (1981) *Wally's Stories*. Cambridge, Mass.: Harvard University Press.

Paley, V. G. (1988) *Bad Guys Don't Have Birthdays*. Chicago: University of Chicago Press.

Paley, V. G. (1990) *The Boy Who Would Be a Helicopter*. Cambridge, Mass.: Harvard University Press.

Papert, S. (1982) *Mindstorms*. Brighton: Harvester Press.

Papousek, H. and Papousek, M. (1987) Intuitive parenting, in J. D. Oakley (ed.) *Handbook of Infant Development*. New York: Wiley.

Parkin, R. (1991) Fair play: children's mathematical experiences in the infant classroom, in N. Browne (ed.) *Science and Technology in the Early Years*. Buckingham: Open University Press.

Pimm, D. (ed.) (1981) *Mathematics, Teachers and Children*. London: Hodder and Stoughton/The Open University.

Pound, L. and Gura, P. (1997) Communities of experts, in P. Gura (ed.) *Reflections on Early Education and Care*. London: British Association for Early Childhood Education.

Pound, L., Cook, L., Court, J., Stevenson, J. and Wadsworth, J. (1992) *The Early Years: Mathematics*. London: Harcourt Brace Jovanovich.

Pugh, G. and De'Ath, E. (1984) *The Needs of Parents*. London: Macmillan.

Read, J. (1992) A short history of children's building blocks, in P. Gura (ed.) *Exploring Learning: Young Children and Blockplay*. London: Paul Chapman.

Rinaldi, C. (1997) A measure for friendship, in M. Castagnetti and V. Vecchi (eds) *Shoe and Meter*. Municipality of Reggio Emilia: Regio Children.

Rogers, J. (1997) Shopping around for answers. *Times Educational Supplement*, 11 July.

Rogoff, B. (1990) *Apprenticeship in Thinking*. Oxford: Oxford University Press.

Rosen, C. and Rosen, H. (1973) *The Language of Primary School Children*. Harmondsworth: Penguin.

Salmon, P. (1988) *Psychology for Teachers*. London: Hutchinson.

School Curriculum and Assessment Authority (1996) *Nursery Education: Desirable Outcomes for Children's Learning on Entering Compulsory Education*. London: SCAA/Department for Education and Employment.

Selleck, D. (1997) Baby Art: art is me, in P. Gura (ed.) *Reflections on Early Education and Care*. London: British Association for Early Childhood Education.

Sharp, C. and Hutchison, D. (1997) How do season of birth and length of schooling affect children's attainment at Key Stage 1? A question revisited. National Foundation for Educational Research – paper received from NFER.

Sinclair, A. (1988) La notation numérique chez l'enfant, in H. Sinclair (ed.) *La production de notations chez le jeune enfant: langage, nombre, rythmes et mélodies*. Paris: Presses Universitaires de France.

Stein, G. (1989) The influence of parents' mathematical experiences on their children's mathematics. MA thesis, University of Surrey.

Stobbs, W. (1968) *The Story of the Three Little Pigs*. Harmondsworth: Penguin.

Sylva, K. (1997) The early years curriculum: evidence based proposals, in *Developing the Primary School Curriculum: the Next Steps*. A collection of papers from an invitational conference held by the School Curriculum and Assessment Authority, 9–10 June 1997. London: SCAA.

Tacon, R. and Atkinson, R. (1997) *Teaching Infants Mental Arithmetic*. Peacehaven County Infant School (pamphlet).

Thumpston, G. (1994) Mathematics in the National Curriculum: implications for learning in the early years, in G. Blenkin and A. V. Kelly (eds) *The National Curriculum and Early Learning*. London: Paul Chapman.

Tizard, B. and Hughes, M. (1984) *Young Children Learning*. London: Fontana.

Tizard, B., Blatchford, P., Burke, J., Farquhar, C. and Plewis, I. (1988) *Young Children at School in the Inner City*. London: Inner London Education Authority.

Trevarthen, C. (1990) Signs before speech, in T. A. Sebeok and J. U. Sebeok (eds) *The Semiotic Web*. Berlin: Mouton de Gruyter.

Vernon Lord, J. (1972) *The Giant Jam Sandwich*. London: Jonathan Cape.

Vygotsky, L. S. (1978) *Mind in Society*. Cambridge, Mass.: Harvard University Press.

Vygotsky, L. S. (1986) *Thought and Language*. Cambridge, Mass.: MIT Press.

Walkerdine, V. (1988) *The Mastery of Reason*. London: Routledge.

Walkerdine, V. (1989) *Counting Girls Out*. London: Virago.

Weir, R. (1962) *Language in the Crib*. The Hague: Mouton.

Wells, G. (1985) *Language Development in the Preschool Years*. Cambridge: Cambridge University Press.

Wells, G. and Nicholls, J. (eds) (1985) *Language and Learning: An Interactional Perspective*. Lewes: Falmer Press.

Whalley, M. (1994) *Learning to Be Strong*. Sevenoaks: Hodder and Stoughton.

Widlake, P. and Macleod, F. (1984) *Raising Standards*. Coventry: Community Education Development Centre.

Williams, H. (1996) Developing numeracy in the early years, in R. Merttens (ed.) *Teaching Numeracy*. Leamington Spa: Scholastic.

Womack, D. (1993) Game, set and match? *Times Educational Supplement*, 8 October.

Wood, D. (1991) Aspects of teaching and learning, in P. Light, S. Sheldon and M. Woodhead (eds) *Learning to Think*. London: Routledge.

Young-Loveridge, J. M. (1987) Learning mathematics. *British Journal of Developmental Psychology*, 5: 155–67.

Young-Loveridge, J. M. (1989) The relationship between children's home experiences and their mathematical skills on entry to school. *Early Child Development and Care*, 43: 43–59.

Index